THEY SENT ME FORTH

THEY SENT ME FORTH

*The Greatest Australian
Story Never Told*

ANGELA M SCIBERRAS

Copyright

Acknowledgement

THE FOLLOWING ACKNOWLEDGEMENT PAYS RESPECT TO THE TRADITIONAL CUS-
TODIANS AND ANCESTORS OF THIS COUNTRY, AND THE CONTINUATION OF THEIR
CULTURAL, SPIRITUAL AND RELIGIOUS PRACTICES. WE RESPECTFULLY ACKNOWL-
EDGE PAST AND PRESENT TRADITIONAL CUSTODIANS OF THIS ENTIRE LAND OF AUS-
TRALIA, AND RESPECT THEIR CULTURE AND IDENTITY, BOUND UP WITH THE LAND
AND SEA FOR GENERATIONS. WE ADVISE ABORIGINAL AND TORRES STRAIT IS-
LANDER VIEWERS THAT THIS BOOK MAY CONTAIN IMAGES OR NAMES OF DECEASED
PEOPLE.

Contents

Dearly Beloved

We are gathered here today to get through this thing called life
Electric word life, it means forever,
and thats a mighty long time.
But I'm here to tell you, there's something else.
The after world...

\- PRINCE

I

CROSSING THE
THRESHOLD

"A human being is born to set out on his quest, like a knight of Arthur's court."

- DOROTHEA MATTHEWS DOOLING

One can never truly comprehend the extent of reach of one act. It will only be in time, that we shall see what the act of telling this story will become. I pray that every word, concept, and symbol will feed your soul, inspire your heart to hope, and fill you with peace — the peace that passes all understanding.

As you read these pages, I hope you feel the love, dedication, and genuine good intention behind every word. In truth I am sobered by the implications of putting these words in front of you, the old saying "the road to hell is paved with good intentions," an oft-quoted warning. There is no need for you to change your thinking or believe a word of what I say. This work exists as an expression of my experience of the truth, and and my perception of what I have been shown. I make it very clear that any person, place or group spoken of within this story are merely pieces in the puzzle of my own path. Just because they are spoken of, does not mean that they align with, or believe any or all of what I say or envision. I did not go on a mission to prove any one theory as correct, just merely followed the crumbs as they came to me, making sense to my journey alone. Just because a reference is used, in no way do I wish to claim that they align or subscribe to my story.

As this work moved through me, I shed many tears of humility and bathed in the energy of unconditional love. In no way does this book exist to make wrong of you or your ancestors, nor persecute in any way. May you feel the love woven between these pages, from myself, and all those on the other side of the veil of this reality. For if this journey has taught me anything, it is that our ancestors and beloveds stand waiting for our return, and more than that, they have never left us.

They Sent Me Forth is the story of the bloodlines of those who came from the tribes of the boats of Avalon. It is the story of my ancestors, and most probably yours. It is the story of a multidimensional plan to heal the past, from a vantage point of the future, linking the limitless dimensions filled with beings who are working with us. I was sent here as a navigator to align my heart to the prompting of pure love and compassionate service. I come to serve as a channel and messenger from my ancestors, some of the first European settlers of Australia. I come to be God's hands and feet.

I commit to bringing healing to the pain caused by and held in my bloodlines. I am charged with a message and its delivery, in the hope of reparation and reconciliation. A small part of the walk towards healing this land Australia. The words of history, spoken and passed through generations, can become spellbinding. They prevent us from growing, having compassion, understanding and being set free from the bonds of old mental constructs and ideologies. We are often unaware of the mental prisons designed to control and keep one small. As much as this matrix we live in has been geared to keep us from evolving, there is metaphysical coding – implanted signs in our reality to override and awaken those who will see. It is time for truth, for revelation, resolution, and regeneration. We must evolve beyond the cycles of pain and suffering, control, and retaliation. Within the blueprint of the Australian and global timeline is a plan, a plan for healing.

This book is a glimpse of an aspect of this blueprint, a multidimensional map of modern myth and truth. A collection of symbols woven to ignite your awareness and explore the vast bounty of expanded states and new realms awaiting us. We are part of a diverse universe of dimensions. Death is but one portal. God speaks to us through all of life's creations, the messages come all the time. The question is whether or not we pick up the Morse code. To some people, Morse code is a series of sounds, meaningless to the untrained ear. To others it is a complex and detailed communication, received and shared. The value and meaning of the message depends on who is hearing it.

It turns out my life, and the lives of the ancestors before me, are a culmination of a dream, dreamed long before, by those dead long before my birth. A dream of sovereignty, love, and peace. Ancestors work together to speak with and through us. Pathways of time are not linear, they are an unfathomable coexistence of past, present, future, and the multiverse running alongside, above and within itself. What people may see as myth, for me has become reality, a living reminder of our greatest and most loving potential. We have for so long forgotten the dreaming that pulsates within our bloodlines and bones.

We are not the ancestors of convicts alone. We are also the ancestors of the tribes of the boats of Avalon, and until we remember the aspects of our greatest selves, we will continue to live within the dream spell that tricks us into believing we are powerless and still in chains—the chains our ancestors removed long ago. The more I walk this journey, and key pieces of information fall into place, the more I can see golden threads that when aligned, collapse timelines, places, and blueprints. They were set up to aid us in fulfilling our destiny, from long before we even realised we had one. The point being, when I looked back over my entire life, every moment, even those I considered off-track, were planned and with hindsight, pivotal. We are gathering on both sides of the veil: experienced, powerful and determined. Poised on an arc of a grand cycle of the future merging with ancient timeframes and myths. The tales of ancestors past and present are melding the fulfilment of our potential future. This myth, this healing, goes far beyond Australia, reaching across the world, still amidst the wake of misuse of British Sovereignty's power.

Stepping through the stones as a time traveller, the ancient stories of King Arthur, Merlin, the Round Table, the Holy Grail, and Excalibur align with this place and time. The symbolism is crying out once more to the ancestors of this bloodline, the ancestors who know this myth within their bones. A signpost for our present and future joining the dots backwards to unlock the puzzle of the past, so that we may declare a glorious future. The greatest story never told is yet to begin. It is the story we will write together – the story our ancestors will tell about us. Write its pages with me.

Angela Mary Sciberras (Shrimpton)

2

THE GREATEST AUSTRALIAN STORY NEVER TOLD

"A great teacher never strives to explain her vision. She invites you to stand beside her and see for yourself."

- THE REV. R. INMAN

At the start of my life, or even the start of my knowledge of my task, I had no thought of being who I am today, nor how I might presume to bring this message. Too young to understand what had happened or how - a pawn on the chessboard of life - my path was unknown, yet inevitable. I imagined I had control over my destiny, yet, as the journey unfolded, I wondered if this was all predestined from the beginning. Was I simply arriving at the pre-determined, pre-planned points in my life?

Destiny, I've learned, is still a choice, though somehow even when we think we are off-track, when joining the dots backwards, every single moment lines up to the same point. Unrelated moments in time, intertwined in the unseen, complex threads of our lives. And therefore, both must be true, both free will and predestination exist. I now understand my job is to choose my life for all it was, and is, and all it wasn't, and isn't. And trust I will find my way whether I think I know where I am going or not.

A true understanding of my destiny evades me. The moment I think I know what it is, I am humbled by the mind-boggling twists and turns I never see coming. It seems the more I know, the more I realise I don't know; the more that's revealed, the more I realise I have one job to do. Follow each tiny crumb, act when I can, and trust. Destiny is a much larger matter, occurring despite our vulnerabilities, failings, and inability to act towards our greatest potential. I may not even see its fulfilment before I leave this world.

If someone had told me when I was young that I would become a kinesiologist, a palliative bedside therapeutic harpist, and a connector to the other worlds, I would have said they were crazy. I would never have believed that my life would go the way it has, and that I would write this book, sharing this message. I can think of nothing more important to say than this. Those who die never leave, and they wish to share a message. There is no more important legacy than to impart what I believe is true. We are never alone.

The ancestors, both mine and many others in their legion, work together to speak with and through me on this path. I now know, even as this task is far from complete, that it is part of the dreaming of my British ancestral legacy, nurtured and recalled so we can again make it real in the minds of all. What some may see as myth, for me has become a reality, a living reminder of our greatest and most loving potential, and so my task begins.

Like all myths, based on some truth, dreams, visions, or tales, they exist to enlighten, to rekindle the universal dream of peace, unity, and love. To remind us of our most profound potential as souls and humans. It's enough for me to know that with every tiny step I am contributing to something far greater than I am aware. I hope in the coming pages, you will see what we are here to complete, together. I am just the messenger. I must pass the baton on, because it takes a village.

We are in a continuum of time having a part to play. Once I have communicated the message, there will be those whose role it will be to develop the knowledge, those who will transform the knowledge to action, and those who will forge the action to create a new reality. I'm called to join the dots backwards to bring healing to the present and hope for our future, a future that moves towards an ever-evolving harmony between all people. We must shed and leave behind the patterns that no longer support our growth, in order to be free.

Poised on an arc of a grand cycle of time, past and future merge, and lifetimes meld in completion. This is a story that blends ancient timeframes and myths and tales of ancestors, for the fulfilment of our potential future. There is a reason we are all alive now, and we cannot dismiss that reason.

As an emissary of light, I commit to helping to begin the spiritual healing of 250 years of compounded pain. By no means do I intend to suggest that my story and its outcomes will bring the end of pain for Australia's First Nations people, but I know I am charged with a message, and with the task of its delivery.

You may interpret this story as just a series of fascinating, colourful tales of the past, or recognise it as a signpost for our future. Join the dots backwards with me to unlock the puzzle of the past to reveal the greatest story that has never been told. In no way do I wish to speak for Aboriginal people, I speak only for myself and my dreaming. I acknowledge that the lore, customs and spiritual heritage of Aboriginal people is vast and varies depending on the country we are on.

3

A FOOT IN BOTH WORLDS

"What if you slept, and what if in your sleep you dreamed, and what if in your dream you went to heaven and there plucked a strong and beautiful flower, and what if when you awoke you had the flower in your hand? Oh, what then?"

- SAMUEL TAYLOR COLERIDGE

Woven into my story is imagination and the mystical, drawn together with symbolism and reality. I have always been in between worlds. As a child, that was the most comfortable place for me. The place that felt unnatural was the earth. Though I grew up on the floor of the Anglican Church, I don't consider myself religious, although I have been spiritual for as long as I can recall. My first encounters with spirits were as a young child. I would see vivid and awake-like dreams almost nightly. I would wake to see a face centimetres in front of mine, having it slowly disappear. I never felt scared, or thought I was in danger. But it did leave my heart racing and mind wondering.

A recurring experience I had as a child was of waking in my little bedroom at the end of our hallway, with my door open and seeing a man who, for years, I assumed was tall as his head reached the beam across the top of the doorway. He was not tall. I saw him for years, not knowing why he was there, and not telling anyone I was seeing him. I never thought much about it until I overheard a conversation between my neighbour and her friend about the man who had hung himself in that doorway. Once I knew his truth, that he'd hung himself, I didn't see him anymore.

Years later, I had another experience. I was a teenager and attended band practice with my brother each Tuesday night. He would come and pick me up or, if I didn't go to band practice, he would come anyway to visit my mother. Most Tuesdays my brother brought his four-year-old son with him.

One Tuesday night, I was unwell. I decided I wouldn't go to practice and stayed in bed instead. I fell asleep early but woke at about 9pm to see a small boy standing in my doorway. If my brother came to visit, it was usually about that time. The boy stood there and stared. In my sleepy state, I assumed it was my nephew, so I called him to come and give me a hug. He then stepped behind my euphonium case near the door to hide. I sat up in bed, amused, "What are you doing, come here?" I said.

He continued to hide, which I thought strange. I turned to pull my covers back and see properly what he was doing, and when I turned back, he wasn't there. I got out of bed and walked down the hall to find my mum, where she often was, sitting in the kitchen near the heater, reading.

"Mum, where are the boys?"

She looked perplexed. "Ange, they didn't come tonight."

"What do you mean?" I asked, "I just saw my nephew in the hallway, I spoke to him."

"No, Ange, that isn't possible. They didn't visit tonight."

I guess I will never know who the boy was, and why he was standing there, but it was among the first of many such experiences in my life. A true turning point in my training came after many years of being visited by spirits, when I met Rosemary. For a long time, I battled horrific dreams filled with visions of black people falling on me in my sleep, seeing blood on my bed, dismembered and injured black people hanging from trees. I would wake in a terrified sweat, but even though I was awake, I would continue to see the blood-soaked people standing around me. There was no escape from the dream, I would wake up with my eyes wide open to see it as if it was reality.

There were times when I thought what was happening to me was demonic; a pastor at the time wondered the same thing as my visions were at times so terrible. Rosemary didn't support that belief. When we met, the door to my life opened wide and changed everything. The meeting was the catalyst for a path of discovery I could never have imagined. I will always be grateful for Rosemary, she has been one of my most cherished friends and guides.

Rosemary invited me to travel down south, to a home perched on the side of a cliff, in beautiful Kiama Downs. Destiny awaited me in a new realm where I did not yet understand what was unfolding. It was very dark when I arrived at the house, no moon in sight, and the loud ocean pounding the cliff wall, sometimes crashing hard enough to shake the foundations. You could feel, smell and hear the sea's power all night long. I woke in the morning and walked into the lounge room to find the curtains were open to a breathtaking and almost uninterrupted view of the ocean. To the left, an enormous pine tree, planted 40 years earlier by the owner's mother, Mary, towered over the house. In its position on the rocks, it stood as a huge sentinel, protecting the house and everyone in it.

In my first days in the house, I couldn't sleep with the lights off. The energy from the world of spirit was so high that I sensed it could reach out and touch me. And it did. I often woke to the sensation of someone touching my legs, pulling the blankets back and touching my face. I slept fitfully; I wasn't afraid, but I couldn't help but feel shock when I was woken. Now, I wish I'd been calm enough to ask them what they wanted. That took years of training and many bumps in the night.

When Mary and Don Davis bought this house, they knew it was a special place. Don had passed away only a few months before Lindy, their daughter, met Rosemary. Lindy invited Rosemary, who was at the time on a strong spiritual path, to stay while her family worked out what they would do with the house. I never met Don and Mary but had seen pictures of them as elderly people. At home one evening, far from the house at the sea, I was in the space between sleep and wakefulness, and my eyes were closed. I sensed someone standing beside the bed.

There had been no one else in the house when I went to bed, but I opened my eyes to see a man with darkish hair, wearing something green, similar to an army outfit. He was leaning over my bed and looking at my face. I sat up screaming. He must have been just as shocked that I could see him, as he jumped back and yelled: "Can you hear me, can you see me?"

I ran down the hallway and curled up in the blue chair in the lounge room. I grabbed the phone and called Rosemary. It was around 11pm. It took me at least half an hour to calm down as I cried and explained to Rosemary what I had seen. "There was a man in my room!" It was the single most profound example of spiritual sight I had ever had. In previous encounters, the people hadn't spoken to me. Sometimes, that was because I was already running and gave them no time. One week later, I would see him again.

I was back in Kiama having dinner with Lindy and her gentle, kind husband Mervyn. One of the most talented and passionate cooks I've ever met, I call him chief of soul food. Mervyn asked if I would like a cup of tea in the lounge room, and nodding thank you, I made my way to the room to find a pinkish coloured leather lounge, and soft blue-grey carpet underfoot. I leaned in to look at the dozens of photos, most of an older man who I recognised from the house on the water. One old colour photo struck me. It was of two or three young men standing in green army outfits, and one man in particular, with darkish hair, had on a green outfit I recognised. It was him. I burst into tears. "Who is the man in that photograph?" I asked.

I was inconsolable, until Lindy, gentle and warm, calmed me down.

"Why? Why do you ask?" she said.

"Well," I sniffed, "I saw that man in my bedroom. It was him, he was there!"

Lindy smiled. "Angela, that's my father, Don." She turned her face to the sky and called out, tongue in cheek, "Dad! Why are you going into young ladies' bedrooms?"

That was my introduction to Don and Mary. A cherished relationship with two souls I never had the pleasure of meeting, yet feel I've known for much longer than this life. While I was at the haven by the sea, I dived into Don's massive library of spiritual material, research and books. It was there I began to understand my gifts and realised it wasn't a bad thing. There wasn't something wrong with me, I just had to be patient and learn how to understand it.

For many years since that profound moment of change, both my husband and I have travelled with Lindy and Mervyn, who are like mentors to us. We have learned the laws of spirit, the art of healing, and dedicated ourselves to the path of love and service. Out of the blue really, Lindy and I studied kinesiology together, and continue using the tools it gives us to do what we can for others. I learned, through their example, how to use the wisdom from following the signs, symbols, and essential confirmations of intuition. Without those, we had no signal of the path. When fear would take over, Lindy would gently remind us it was often at the 59th minute of the 11th hour that spirit would show its card, and the answer would reveal itself.

I learned to trust in things I couldn't see or control. I could read, hear, and follow the breadcrumbs spirit would leave. For while we can be open to guidance, we do also have and need our free will. Those in spirit know they can't give us all the answers. How boring this incredible life would be, if we had the answers ahead of time! There would be no need to develop the tools of spirit: unconditional love, trust, courage, faith, and service. I learned that when I asked for courage, and to learn to trust, spirit would bring me circumstances filled with fear, terror, or an unknown path. The feeling of being lost was my first response. At those times, I imagined myself as an acrobat, walking the wire with no aid; if I fell, I would die.

As I put the finishing touches on this book, I realised I was fast approaching the point where I could no longer turn back. Had I given up, had I not followed my inner guidance, truth, or path, I knew I would soon become miserable beyond description. Once we extend ourselves into taking that step, waking up to the greater purpose of our life, no matter how afraid we may be, we can never go back. Whenever I have tried to walk away I have felt as if something inside me was dying; as if I was leaving the promised land and turning my back on the mountain I'd almost climbed. I would have been giving away my heritage; I would have been trying to forget a great promise I once gave.

I'm weaving a quilt from the fabric of my life, my ancestors' lives and history, to stretch across different levels of reality and time. I hope the spiritual sharing in this book can remind you that your journey is sacred and awaken you to story and myth and the knowledge that all our lives are a quest and adventure. Love never fails. It is one cosmic force. It overcomes all obstacles and is the fabric of miracles. It is the greatest power in the universe. Love never, ever dies.

4

THE QUEST

"When you want something, the whole universe conspires to help you."

- PAULO COELHO

In telling this story, drawing together a lifetime of synchronicity, mystical connections and adventures, I have come to believe that I have a reason to be here. Part of that reason is to deliver a message from the past: they wish to make things right. They don't want the pain of the past to pass on to our children's children.

This message is unfolding, through signs and symbols, through of some of the greatest souls who have lived on this planet. They wish to share the truth, it is time to make things right. In the telling of this story, I hope to prove that those who pass never die; that they are around us, guiding us, helping us, and hoping we hear them. I hope to prove that miracles are possible and more than that, probable when we take a powerful stand for something greater than ourselves.

I have been afraid to tell this story, and not least is the trepidation about allowing the world into what could be perceived as a white man's circus. But I have embraced the privilege of telling it and getting the job done. What is the job? The job is for us to understand our part in history; to connect to our compassion and forgiveness for the greater good of our children's children. To break the cycle of retribution and suffering, hear our ancestor' call to end the pain and ignite the possibility of forgiveness, love and peace.

You will notice the word possibility throughout this book, so I will explain the context from which I use the word. The most transformational and powerful use of the word possibility comes from Werner Erhard. "We think of possibility as options, and while true, possibility has a much deeper subconscious message in which it can allude to what is permissible. I am sure if we inspect, when using the word possibility, we are operating inside an existing paradigm that tells us whether something is achievable."

So, in saying this, I am committed to the word being listened to in the way Werner perceives its power to be. He explains that to create possibility is to bring forward a domain in which new options become possible. So, it's not finding new options within the same range; it is producing a whole new range of options. When these alternative possibilities are created, you will be at the cause of their being brought into existence, along with a few a miracles, and that is the domain of God.

It is time to break the barriers of pain and fear that hold us back from experiencing the awe and wonder of unity and love. Taking this stand will affect our future, and we do it for the sake of healing the past and present. For the possibility that we can be the hands and feet of God and our ancestors, to help them make the past right so we can stand on stronger ground. In doing that, we are acting for the sake of tomorrow.

It is important to understand that the past is not my fault, nor is it yours. What happened to the First Nations people after our ancestor's arrival in 1788 is horrific, unfathomable. But blame and guilt have never had the power to heal. Another term I thought vital to discuss is the word responsibility, a word scattered through the pages of this book. For the sake of clear communication and alignment with the philosophies of Werner Erhard once again, I do not cast blame or guilt, but take the view that if we can be responsible for our life history and circumstance, we are then cause in the matter of our life. Being cause in the matter of our life gives us the power to change it. Werner Erhard says if we take the barriers, pretences, and those things we didn't take responsibility for out of the way, what we have left is love.

Where will this stone, thrown into the pond of time, land? I often wonder how the ripples will move out into the world. I have shed more tears in writing this book than I could ever explain and now hand it to you with an open heart and grateful soul. As I look back over my journey, I see one common thread. It has taken half my life, and the ability to look back and join the dots to see I am moved by the possibility of the unity of humanity through the arts and creativity.

I write, seeking to recreate my experience of living this story. I have been clueless to the connections of the many and varied aspects of this pathway, and it wasn't until, when joining all the seemingly unconnected events, experiences and people, that I could see the golden thread that moved through and connected everyone. What I can assure you is that even though you may feel lost for a moment in these pages, it will at some point make sense, just like it did for me. I lived this story while never seeing the next piece of the puzzle coming. Know you're on the right track, even when it feels as if you are not.

5

SIGNS, SAINTS & SYNCHRONICITY

"Saints are real, and they are very close to us."

- CAROLYNE MYSS

I would have rejected any suggestion that saints were real. In fact, it never interested me, nor did I understand the concept of saints in the way many others might. Not only do they exist, but I could — and did — communicate with them.

Liz, a kinesiology client, had a traumatic time caring for her parents who both passed away from cancer. She also had cancer herself. On the day she found out she was in remission, she got news that her husband, Tony, had cancer. Tony died a short time later. A caring sister, Liz made an appointment to see me to find out who the kinesiologist was that her brother had been raving about.

Liz had been left with an immense burden of loss and grief having cared for and lost her most beloved people. Liz was my teacher in so many ways. Accomplishing what many refuse, she committed to the journey of self-discovery with dedication and an understanding that it could take time to heal such wounds. For the past ten years and with more kinesiology sessions than I could count, I have worked with Liz. Each of her sessions profound, it wasn't too long into our journey when the tenor of the sessions changed. We both noticed it, and it took us a while to work out exactly what was happening.

Such dramatic changes don't happen to most of my clients. Neither of us were manipulating the sessions in any way (conscious or unconscious) to an intended outcome. The change happened of its own accord. With rigorous observation and repeated incidents, what became clear was that Liz's late husband, Tony, was sending messages through the muscle testing. This seemed so out of the ordinary that we spent a long time verifying and questioning the messages, analysing the dynamics of the sessions, and closely observing what happened during the kinesiology sessions before we agreed: there were messages from an external source. That source was Tony. Once we trusted that it was possible and true, things became really interesting.

On one occasion Liz came to my clinic and I welcomed her in the usual way. She sat while I took a few things from inside my black Chinese cupboard, a beautiful piece of furniture covered in gold and red butterflies, and flowers. It is ancient looking, and one of my favourite things. As I opened it, a box all but leapt out, spilling its contents. The little white box was, until then, not only sealed, but when I tried to open it previously, I'd struggled. My attempts came to nothing. Yet, today, with Liz in the room, it opened of its own accord, its contents strewn across the floor.

Inside the box were five hundred business cards with my details on the front and, on the back, the most beautiful red roses. They fell in such a way that every single one landed with the rose side up and covered almost every part of the floor in front of us. Embarrassed, I knelt down to collect them, apologising as I passed. I didn't even get to pick up more than a couple when Liz interrupted.

"Stop." She said. "Stop what you're doing, look at this."

I sat down on my chair, facing her to see what she had in her hands.

"Angela, you will not believe this," she said. "I woke up this morning and was doing some clearing of one of my parents' cupboards and this little booklet fell out of the shelf in front of me." She passed the booklet to me, saying, "Look at the floor, and now read this."

On the cover of this little pamphlet, filled with red roses was the Miraculous Invocation to St. Therese:

O Glorious St. Therese,
Whom Almighty God has raised up to aid
And inspire the human family,
I implore your Miraculous Intercession.
You are so powerful in obtaining every need,
Of body and spirit from the Heart of God.
Holy Mother Church proclaims you Prodigy of Miracles,
The greatest saint of modern times.
Now I beseech you to answer my petition
And to carry out your promises of
Spending heaven doing good on earth.
Of letting fall from Heaven a Shower of Roses.
Little Flower give me your childlike faith
To see the Face of God
In the people and experiences of my life,
And to love God with full confidence.
Amen.

We both sat, mouths open, looking at the floor. Liz was about to bring up what happened to her with the little booklet of St. Therese when I opened the cupboard door. Out flew a shower of roses, almost from heaven. This was the beginning of the showers of roses from St. Therese, and my first experience with this saint and witnessing her work with Liz and me on our journey. Miraculous moments happened over and over; a flood of signs, as if once they knew we were receiving them, it was game on.

A pertinent story, and one we love, is the session around selling Liz's house and her decision on where to move to. Though we'd balanced out many fears, old beliefs and issues around what she thought was possible, she was still unsure.

"Ok," I asked, "so where are you thinking of moving to?"

"I like the area where my late husband and I used to have coffee and attend a beautiful church from time to time, I also would like somewhere near or on the water maybe?"

"Ok, fine, let's do some balancing around that." Just as I turned to begin the work, my doorbell rang. I rarely leave a session to open the door unless I am expecting something, but no one else was present to open the door. I turned to Liz, "I don't know why, but I feel I need to go answer that." On opening the door, I found a man with a big glossy brochure. He was a real estate agent and the properties in the brochure were waterside properties.

"Thought you might like to see some properties on the water," he said. "Have a nice day!" And he walked off.

Two things were intensely odd about the entire event. First, we lived nowhere near these water properties and second, it's most unusual for agents to go door-to-door to hand out promotional material. If I didn't have Liz there to witness it, no one would have believed me. Gob smacked, I walked back into the room and slapped the leaflet in front of her. "Right," I said, laughing. "What more evidence do you need that you can have whatever it is you wish for?"

Liz found her perfect home closer to the water, a rose garden out the front, moments from her favourite church and within walking distance to the coffee shops she and Tony loved.

I will share a last story that showed us both the beauty of a relationship that continues even after a loved one has passed. In the moments before Liz was to sell her house, as with many of us, confusion and fear set in. On the day of our session surrounding the sale, St. Therese was on the agenda. Liz decided she'd light a candle when she got home, place a red rose in front of it and say the prayer to St. Therese asking for a miracle.

She bought a bunch of red roses on the way home, and that night had a moment of tears and frustrated conversation with Tony. It centred on her feeling left alone and afraid. She completed the Prayer of St. Therese and then pleaded with Tony for help to sell the house. With that, Liz blew the candle out. As she did, the phone rang.

"Hello, Liz speaking."

"Hi Liz, my name is Tony."

Silence. Liz thinking, oh my God, he is quick!

"Yes, she said, how can I help you?"

"Well, I was hoping I could help you." He paused for a few seconds, then continued. "I'm a property manager and a friend of a friend said you might need some guidance to ensure you get the best outcome for your property. Also, I hear you've been through quite a lot ... so I'd love to help you."

An unexpected call brought a Tony. He helped her sell for a good price. Liz and Tony taught me the power of genuine love; that love never dies. Tony has been present and continued to walk this journey — her Guardian Angel — even since he passed. Time nor death cannot unbind love. This precious time with Liz was training us both to understand the communications from the departed in the people, moments and symbols all around us. Sometimes it is through the tiny, seemingly insignificant signs that, once seen, reveal the next steps on the map of the blueprint of our mission. Like dots connecting forwards and backwards in ways we couldn't imagine possible.

My walk with Liz is private, though she was deeply happy to allow me to share this tiny part of her miraculous creation a life that is unrecognisable and profound. Liz's life now inspires me every day. She has transformed her pain and loss into more power and self-expression than either of us could have conceived in those first few sessions. My relationship with Liz started my journey of reading the signs from the other side. There were many in my journey, particularly when I began working at the bedside of the dying as a therapeutic harpist.

Chris was brought to see me a few months before passing away from bowel cancer. His son whispered, "Good luck," to me as he walked into my rooms. A man of few words, Chris rarely opened up to anyone. I saw him weekly, and there was the tenor of the story *Tuesdays with Morrie*, though for us it was Fridays with Chris. Some days he was great, filled with energy, and other days his pain and suffering was excruciating. Yet he would talk about his life, his mistakes, his regrets, his joys. We talked about what it was like to die, and he was open and brave enough to allow me to ask the hard questions that many feel afraid to ask. Sharing from the heart, he told me his deep truths. A week before he died, while he was still lucid and communicating, I asked him for a favour; I wanted him to promise that he'd give me a sign from the other side.

"Ok, love," he said, in his beautiful English accent that I can still hear ringing in my ears. I asked him to make sure it was clear, something I wouldn't miss.

"Go on girl," he said, "I will."

Every single time I visited, Chris and I would talk about Ned Kelly steak. This conversation would unfold as I was massaging his feet with sacred oils. Cancer patients don't have much of an appetite, but in the last few weeks of his life, Chris's appetite returned. His son would head to the local butcher and get a few "Ned Kelly" steaks — huge T-Bone steaks, cooked to Chris' liking and served with sauce, mashed potato and veggies. Every week, Chris would describe these meals with great enthusiasm.

This dear soul, surrounded by his loving family, passed away in his son's arms, loved and at peace. I was blessed to spend time with him the day before he died, jumping into his bed and sitting up beside him after playing harp from the corner of the room. This time I didn't do his feet, as I had every week past. He hadn't responded or spoken for a couple of days and we all felt it would soon be his time. Leaning in, I spoke to him as I always did, and how he always had to me. "How the bloody hell are ya, mate?"

And with that he motioned and groaned. Everyone spun around, shocked that he was still in there.

"Hey, how are you I said?"

He groaned again, but I couldn't quite get what he was saying.

"Ok, mate," I said, "I can't understand a word you are saying, what is it?"

And he said frustrated, but also trying to laugh, "Where's my bloody foot rub?"

Well, we all burst out laughing. His son moved to the kitchen to get him a beer and give him a few mouthfuls. His family was so happy to have him relating to them once more, a few more moments together before his final mile home was complete. He died the next day, and I received a message from his son saying he passed peacefully in the early hours of the morning.

In the days to follow, they asked me to play the harp at his funeral. I arrived early, spent some time with Chris, and prepared myself to play. His funeral was the first I'd attended where the curtains at the end of the chapel were closed, then reopened for a standing ovation and encore at the end of the service. Who doesn't, after completing the most important performance of all life, deserve a standing ovation! It was the best funeral I have ever attended. On the way home it was drizzling. I thought of Chris, and our chat about him reaching out and letting me know he was still there and ok. Just as I took the exit, I came to a stop behind a line of cars waiting to turn. A thought crossed my mind, where are you now Chris? I looked up to see on the back of the car directly in front of me a huge sticker on the back window.

The decal — large, was a picture of Ned Kelly, brandishing two pistols, with a caption, "Such is life." For months, Ned Kelly pictures, tattoos, you name it, would show up in the most random moments where I was to decide about an important part of the journey. Ned would be there. For some time after he died, I had vivid dreams where Chris would appear, and some were integral in situations still playing out here on earth. I will always be grateful for what he taught me about the journey of the good death. He allowed me to ask him more than I should have, always answering with way more than I deserved.

My friend has helped guide me in some of my darkest hours, and I know I'll see him again one day. Chris taught me how to be a practitioner at the deathbed, and I believe he prepared me to meet another of my guides, a deep and wise woman who would touch my life immensely and guide me on to Uluru. It was this woman who would give me the sign of the stars, or the Southern Cross. During this very special lady's last mile we had a powerful conversation about death and where we go after we die. When we had all but finished, I asked her if when she died, we could do an experiment.

"Well, yes, I guess so, how?"

"Well, when it's appropriate, can you prove I'm right? That we don't die. That we still go on after we pass. Can you give me a sign, something that is you, to let me know you made it?"

"Yes," she said with a smile, "I will."

Driving home after playing harp at her funeral I travelled the same route I had taken after Chris's funeral. It was raining again. I pulled off onto the same exit, and as I did, I again wondered, how would she make herself known? Like ground hog day, In front of me was a large car, and on its back window was a huge Eureka Stockade flag sticker. It couldn't be, this is way too strange, but the hair on the back of my neck stood up, and I felt a presence. There's only one way to find out if this is something that would symbolise her and get through to those who love her before she made it across the rainbow bridge. I got my phone out and wrote a text to her son, a lovely man who ended up calling me White Lighter, and I called him Way Shower.

"Ok, Way Shower, your mum has sent a message, would it be ok to send you a picture of something to see if it makes any sense to you at all?"

I sat back after clicking send, thinking, oh my god, I shouldn't have done that, they are going to think I am crazy. Time passed by, no response. Silence.

Still no response, and I texted again apologising, telling him not to take any notice it was probably nothing. I worried that I had upset the family with my message. I sent another text apologising. This time receiving a message back.

"No, White Lighter, you haven't upset us, we are all in shock. You won't believe what I am about to tell you. Angela, what you don't know is that our mother loved a band called The Bushwhackers. The Eureka Stockade flag is their symbol. Once, we took Mum on a trip to where Ned Kelly died. The day ended in an argument because she wanted to buy us T-shirts with exactly that symbol on them. We didn't want to wear them, but she wasn't hearing it!"

There was no way I could have known that information. Those on the other side spoke regularly with decals on the back of cars, me often looking up to see Ned Kelly pointing two barrels at my face with the words "Such is life" printed above it. Usually on days I was struggling with things and needed a little nudge to remind me I wasn't alone.

Renowned author Paulo Coelho shares his thoughts on the matter of universal language and sums it up perfectly. He tells us that the universe, spirit, God, however you see it, speaks to us through omens and signs. If we pay attention to the little things, we will see that these signs are everywhere around us. This has been my experience. I imagine that the more universal energy knows how to get our attention, the more we see the signs, note them, and act on them, the more they reveal themselves.

Over the years, I have had people ask me to teach them the language of the universe. While it's flattering on some level, I subscribe to the idea that, as Paulo Coelho makes clear, one cannot teach another how to communicate and read the signs, we can only learn ourselves. So, how can we learn? Coelho advises that we can only "learn this language by making mistakes and daring."

These stories are a tiny drop in the bucket of hundreds of experiences I have had in this way over my lifetime. Maybe I came into this world with a natural ability to see the signs. Though ability aside, there have been many years of developing and honing the skill to where seeing and reading signals has become second nature and my natural way of experiencing life. In fact, when I don't experience the miracles and omens, I notice how quiet the universe has become and wonder why they have ceased. Can I control the omens I hear you ask? No, that is the essence of the miraculous. That is the domain of the divine.

There is, I have learned, a vast difference between intention-setting, manifestations and the miraculous. In my experience planning, intention-setting, and miracles have no relationship. Stepping into the realm of miracles feels like riding by the seat of your pants, heading for a cliff in a car with no brakes, trusting that at the 11th hour, 59th minute something you never imagined happening, will happen. Breakthroughs have often happened in moments of stillness, or when I have been at my lowest, and also in the moments I least expected them.

That is the nature of the miraculous, and why it leaves us awe-struck like a bolt of lightning from heaven. In no way have I intended any part of this story, it has led me, and shown me the way. I can promise that anything I could think up would pale compared to the greater force than I. I know that no matter how many stories I tell, no matter how hard I try to convince, many will remain sceptical. And that's how it should be. There are some things that can only be known through experience. My gift to you is the knowledge that miracles are possible. The rest is up to you.

6

ALL ABOUT A BONNET

"With your personal destiny, you are always guided to meet the right person, at the right moment."

- PAULO COELHO

On 14 December 1996, a package arrived in a brown paper envelope from Surrey, England, to my father's doorstep in Grenfell, NSW. The return address contained a name my father had never heard of, Valda, although her last name was his own. My father called me, excited to share the news of a package of documents "all the way from England."

Inside was information tracing our family line back to the first settlers of this nation. Before Valda Shrimpton, we knew nothing of the extent of our family tree, and its pathway back to the First and Second Fleet and settlers of modern Australia. This piece of snail mail with pictures of my past would be central in the unfolding of my entire life. It would affect the very direction of my future. Valda would never imagine the gigantic impact of her decision to find my father – the next piece in her family tree puzzle - and me youngest daughter in my father's line. That year, I was 19 and had just moved to Sydney to follow my dreams of completing a music degree at the University of Western Sydney.

The Sydney I lived in then was the same location that my ancestors came to, but the monumental differences between their arrival and mine, were hard to fathom. However, as I read of those intrepid travellers, my ancestors, I imagined. Mary was born in 1761, from what we can tell, at Diddlebury in Shropshire, England, under the name of either Davis or Bishop (both are common in the area). It seems my fourth-generation grandmother got herself into some trouble in 1785 when she broke into a house to steal a copper kettle and clothing. On 12 March 1785, 24-year-old Mary was found guilty at Shrewsbury, and sentenced to death by hanging. However, on 31 January 1787, Mary got orders to prepare herself, and after a wagon journey to Gravesend, she boarded the Lady Penrhyn, one of the First Fleet vessels.

The Lady Penrhyn's journey from England was characterised by a severe lack of food and clean water, illness and profound suffering, all common experiences on the ships transporting convicts to the colonies. The ship arrived at Sydney Cove in the dark, with 101 women and more than 70 crewmen cramped into the 30-metre by 8-metre vessel. Down below, the convicts were constrained in tiny cells. Some were further restrained with chains and had endured floggings and punishment with thumbscrews. I marvel at the details of the life of this woman, such a significant forerunner to the lives of my family and me in modern Australia.

Trying to imagine what your ancestors were like is such a difficult undertaking, but much has been written about the First Fleet's journey to help paint the picture of those eight months of her life. The cells below deck were so small that there was not enough room to lie down to sleep. I cannot imagine eight months crouching, kneeling, possibly chained up, among rats, roaches and lice. The putrid cells, buckets for toilets and dirt upon filth, with no way to see outside, breathe fresh air, or even move freely. The experience would never leave you.

Mary Davis Bishop and the women on the Lady Penrhyn stepped onto the shores to what we now call Sydney Harbour in February 1788.

Imagine how it would have been to arrive into Sydney Cove after a gruelling voyage from England. Step onto the solid ground of this great, unfamiliar southern land with nothing but the rags on your back, food to last a few weeks, no shelter, no idea how you would survive. This was not anything like the bustling industrial towns of England; just the quiet shores of an unknown land. Unknown, but not uninhabited. I doubt the people on these fleets of ships had any capacity to imagine the devastating outcome that would befall the people already living in Australia as a result of their arrival. They would have been too consumed with trying to ensure their own survival.

Fast forward 220 years after Mary arrived on Australian soil, early January 2008, I received a email from a woman named Christina Henry. I am not entirely sure how she found me, as I had only been playing harp for a year or two at most. But the email arrived, an invitation to play the harp at an event Christina was organising at St John's Cathedral in Parramatta. I didn't realise, until doing a little more research, that many of my settler descendants were married in the same church all those years ago. Here before me was an invitation to attend an event in honour of the convict women of Australia, The Blessing of the Bonnets. There was an opportunity for descendants of the convict women to attend and present a tribute, in the form of a bonnet they had made, to remember the women who are still largely shrouded in this part of Australia's history.

Christina specifically wished to honour and symbolically remember the lives of the transported women and their children. The Blessing of the Bonnets service was part of a powerful project that she created named Roses from the Heart, and a memorial connected to it that has been displayed all over the world. The bonnet was chosen as the symbol for the project because women were assigned to work as domestics in their unknown land. Each bonnet was created individually and donated to the project by women from Ireland, Britain, Australia and New Zealand. Although created from a template, the maker had the freedom to select their own white or cream fabric and form of embellishment. If they had no connection to any of the women, they could 'adopt' a convict and create their own personal tribute. Each bonnet bears the name of the convict, and many also have the name of the ship on which she travelled.

Christina states that each bonnet commemorates the value of a female convict's life. Made individually, rather than mass-produced, each one symbolises the individuality of the woman whose name it carries. I have heard a rumour that almost 28,000 bonnets were created.

So I, the descendant of Mary Davis Bishop, arrived at St John's Cathedral Parramatta on Thursday, 10 April 2008, my harp in hand. Entering the Cathedral, I found my place at the front of the building and set up for the ceremony. As I have many times before, I pulled out my little Stoney End harp, tuned her and waited for the proceedings to begin. As I sat, Christina handed me a little white handmade bonnet, so I too could take part in the ceremony. It didn't occur to me until that moment that I should have prepared and brought my own bonnet, for Mary.

I did not understand how profoundly moving this ceremony would be. A small antique boat was positioned at the front of the church. As the service began, a long line of women stood up and walked to the little boat, placing their handmade bonnet inside, along with a rose. One-by-one the names of the convict women were read out, and as their descendant, heard their name, they walked to the little boat in their honour, some in tears, some sobbing, some in quiet contemplation, and others gently smiling with the grace of the moment.

I played harp, intuitively, as I do, for an hour or more, as name after name was presented, passing us by like feathers in the breeze. Women who travelled across the seas, some raped and beaten on the journey, arriving to experience the worst the new colony of New South Wales had to offer. It was so moving to see hundreds of women, ancestors of these brave souls standing together in solidarity and pride at the courage it must have taken to be sent to this place and survive. Some did not make it. Some like Mary had relatively successful and full lives in the world.

I couldn't imagine what it must have been like in this church 200 years ago. Timelines began to weave in and out of each other. The now sealed roads became dust, I heard the commotion and bustle of the horse and cart, Parramatta phased in and out of its historical beginnings. I wondered what it would have been like the day before the First Fleet arrived. A wild, vast and beautiful paradise, only the sound of the footsteps of the original people, the words of their songs, the beat of clap sticks, the silence. And the sounds of country. It was a strange feeling to mourn such pioneering souls, while hanging my head with the sadness and shame of what the success of the colony had meant. The destruction of this country's first people and their way of life.

As the line of women dwindled, I was approached by someone who handed me a rose and suggested that as the last few women placed their tribute, I could take my leave from the harp and make my own way up to the front of the church to place my bonnet and rose as a tribute to Mary. And so, as the last couple of women stood silently at the boat, which now overflowed with little white bonnets, I thought about Mary. I thought about all the women connected to me, standing in a line back to Ireland, Britain and Wales.

I lifted my hands from the harp and in silence walked down the long aisle towards the little white boat at the front of the church. What I wasn't ready for was the wave of emotion that hit me, and so many others, as we approached that boat. The ceremony felt sacred, I felt the energy of the past collide with the present and could see in my mind's eye thousands of convict women filling the room, watching on in gratitude and wonder. The room seemed to fill with light, a beam landing on the mountain of bonnets from the past. I stood in front of the boat, and as I lifted my bonnet and placed my rose, I heard the master of ceremonies read the name: Mary Davis Bishop. There she was, standing in front of me, on the other side of the boat, her hands outstretched, reaching through the veil.

"I am here. I am with you, and the journey has just begun. If I survived what I did, how much will you overcome, my daughter. Be strong."

It would be many years later that I would look back on this day and see how divinely timed it was, that even then they were reaching through to speak to me, find me and show me the path. It just took me a while before the penny dropped, and they could breathe a sigh of relief that all their hard work on their side of the veil, to connect, communicate, lead, guide and line up the synchronistic moments, had been noticed. The timeline closed, the vision in my mind ended, and I found myself in silence, standing alone, and quickly turning around to make my way back to my seat.

7

RICHARD SHRIMPTON

"The theft of a black gelding, settled for 5 pounds 10 shillings, was the price you paid to secure a front-row seat in the unfolding of this great nation. Built on the foundation of one of the greatest genocides the world has never known."

- ANGELA SCIBERRAS

On the 11th of June 1789, a man named Richard Shrimpton was sent to the prison hulk The Lion in Portsmouth, and on 29 November 1789, he was prepared to board The Scarborough of the Second Fleet. Hulks were decommissioned ships, afloat but incapable of going to sea, that were used as floating prisons in the 18th and 19th centuries due to a complete lack of room for any more prisoners in the atrociously overcrowded gaols on land. So, instead, most convicts spent their last months in Britain in atrociously overcrowded gaols floating on harbours.

And so, the Second Fleet of six ships left England on 19 January 1790: Lady Juliana and the Guardian, had left earlier, but Justinian, Suprize, Neptune, and Scarborough sailed together. The Guardian struck ice near the Cape of Good Hope and returning to southern Africa, was wrecked on the coast. Stocked with provisions, she was a great loss. Barbara Turner wrote in the Sydney Cove Chronicle on 30 June 1790, that at last the transports had arrived, but the conditions of the convicts was diabolical. The over-crowded and squalid conditions meant 26% of convicts died on the way to Sydney Cove. Turner said the condition of those who were still alive at the time of the landing "could not fail to horrify those who watched."

It is all the more remarkable then that Richard survived to be granted a conditional pardon in November 1797, and two years later in November 1799 he received a 50-acre land grant in the eastern farm district, said to be on modern-day Quarry Road and Bridge Road, next to the Macquarie University. A waterway in the area now bears the name Shrimpton's Creek. In 1802 Richard was cultivating an acre of wheat and six acres of maze, holding 10 bushels of wheat and 20 of maze. He and his wife Ann were childless and used 2 freemen and a convict for labour. [1]

Richard managed a further 50 acres owned by Lieutenant William Kent, of which he had sown 30 in wheat and maize, while caring for 7 horses, 125 sheep, and 20 hogs that belonged to the officer. In 1807, Richard sold that farm and he eventually farmed the richer soils of the Hawkesbury. As was common in the day, after the death of his first wife, Richard married for the second time, to Charlotte Crab, Mary Davis Bishop's daughter. Charlotte Crabb is shown on the colony's 1814 muster as free on the stores, with three children to James Crabb. James seems to disappear from the records just after that and Charlotte was accepted as a widow on 9 August 1819. [2]

After returning to her mother's home at Parramatta, she met Richard Shrimpton, and they were married at St John's Church of England Parramatta. Together, they had four children. The first, Edward Francis, was born in Parramatta in 1819. The family then moved to a farm at Wilberforce where the next three children were born: Charles in 1822, Leah in 1824, and Richard in 1826. However, all the hardship Richard had endured in his life had taken its toll, and he died on his farm on 11 July 1827. He was buried at Wilberforce Cemetery on 12 July

1827, relatively young for our times at only 65 years of age, but perhaps an impressive age for any survivor of the Second Fleet.

When he died, Charlotte inherited the land, all cleared and cultivated, plus one horse, later selling and moving to an area near Bowen Mountain and Kurrajong with her mother, my First Fleet ancestor Mary Davis Bishop. Mary died at Charlotte's home on 1 January 1839 and was buried five days later at St Peter's Church Richmond. At 80 years old, she was a fair age for such a time in history, and considering all she had endured in her lifetime. Charlotte lived until 5 September 1851, when she too died at her home at Kurrajong, and was buried three days later at St Peter's Church, Richmond. She was interred with her mother Mary.[3]

It was only in April 2021 that I learned where the land Mary and Charlotte owned in Bowen Mountain was. It was so moving to walk this still mostly public land to see a huge Norfolk Pine tree stretching its branches to the sky. As my friend Renee and myself collected pine cones scattered on the ground we wondered; did Mary and Charlotte plant these monumental Norfolk Pine trees in honour of Charlottes birth on Norfolk Island? Did my ancestors relax under its bow? I would be nice to think so. Through Richard, Mary, and Charlotte, I connect to the many, and the many wish to send a message. It is time to make things right.

8

THE SQUEAKY WHEEL

"You want to be successful; the universe is helping you."

\- PAULO COELHO

"Hey," said my father, "I had the hairs stand up on the back of my neck right here!" It was 2003 and we were at Wilberforce Cemetery, looking for Richard Shrimpton's grave. Dad was shouting back at me from one part of the cemetery. We had walked between the many old headstones and artworks of the early masons with my sister and her family, all of us together on an adventure to find Richard Shrimpton, our Second Fleet ancestor.

"I feel like he is buried right in this spot, I can feel it!" Dad exclaimed. And who knows? Maybe he did. My father wasn't spiritual, so his reaction showed how strong it must have been for him to notice and be brave enough to say he had. Dad burst out laughing; his usual response when he was shocked and excited about something. We eventually made our way back to my sister's four-wheel-drive and piled in, ready to move on to Richmond to visit the graves of Mary Davis Bishop and her daughter Charlotte. As we attempted to drive off, we realised that even though the car was revving, we weren't going anywhere. Even with more acceleration, we were stuck.

"What the heck is happening," my sister exclaimed, jumping out to have a look. Wandering around the car, we found the back of the four-wheel drive caught on a tree stump. Laughing, as we all do in our family at these oddities, we all jumped out. The car could move forward now that it was relieved of all our weight. We were free. Yet, when we spoke of how we'd gotten stuck on the tree stump, we unanimously decided that Richard didn't want us to leave that day.

Recounting the story now, I wonder whether Richard was there; whether it was our guides and ancestors trying to reach us. Many years passed after that first experience. At that time, I did not know about the Wesleyan section across the road from the cemetery. I had no idea of the role it would play in our future. After one of many two-hour phone conversations with Dad about Richard not having a headstone, we decided it was time to do whatever it took to have him commemorated. We wanted a monument that would be there for us to visit, but also for the generations to come after us.

Many years passed, and in 2016 I completed the Self Expression and Leadership Program as a coach. Part of the requirements of this course was to complete a project, while coaching and supporting others to undertake their own project within the community. I decided to take on the project of organising to have a headstone placed on Richard Shrimpton's grave.

On Monday, 4 July 2016 at 5.38pm, I sent my first email to Hawkesbury Council. I noted the time. I wanted to introduce myself, and ask what I might need to do, or who I might need to talk to, to install a plaque or headstone to acknowledge Richard and mark his place in the cemetery. The reply confirmed what we already suspected. Richard Shrimpton was buried there, but there was no way to locate him. I learned that Richard's first wife, Ann Shrimpton, was also buried there in an unmarked grave. When my first attempt produced nothing more concrete than this basic information, I kept emailing.

It took quite a while for someone in the Council to take me the least bit seriously, but I was determined to find some way to acknowledge my ancestor; to make it known to my family and others who might be interested, that there lay Richard Shrimpton. Though I hadn't intended to make my request public to anyone but the Council, by the time I heard from them, I also had people from nowhere, it seemed, reaching out to me asking for my help to have their ancestors, also buried in Wilberforce Cemetery, acknowledged. Word had gotten around about my project and it was soon clear that I was not the only family member looking for recognition of their ancestors, buried in unmarked graves.

The project was growing; I felt it wanting to become more than just me fulfilling my father's dream of placing a headstone on our ancestor's grave. It sounds crazy, but somehow I could sense, even see the many unmarked souls crowding around me, and making it clear they wanted to be remembered.

I had sleepless nights were I heard these voices whispering, asking me for their help. "Ok, fine!" I sighed. "You can all get recognised! Now can you all stop harassing me?" And, for a time, I imagined them satisfied that their message had gotten through.

I travelled back to Wilberforce Cemetery to connect with the land, and it was then I saw it. I'd not noticed it before, but there was the bush block across the road. The Wesleyan Section – a diamond-shaped piece of land around a half an acre – bordered by enormous sandstone boulders. It seemed they were guarding the block. At the front, through an opening made from large, old-fashioned, wooden beams, was a pathway, 100 metres long, straight to the middle. The path was lined with gum trees, sentinels drawing us to the centre. There, a circle-shaped area revealed itself. As I stood, a potent energy came over me. A huge eagle joined me overhead. The cockatoos screeched, jumping from tree to tree, circling as I approached.

In the book she co-authored with Hamilton Hill, *The Standing Stones Speak: Messages from The Archangels Revealed*, Natasha Hoffman says humanity has forgotten many things we need to know. Of those, three things — our origins, archangels and their presence, and the purpose of the standing stones — are the most important. These great stones and urban mounds often held the bones of the first important ancestors. A combination of temple and tomb.

Natasha Hoffman goes onto say that megaliths are seen as activators and visual reminders of cosmic forces. They act a little like acupuncture needles in the earth's surface, maintaining and stimulating vital energy where it is needed. Once this part of the journey fell into place and became clear for me, I heard from a council representative who seemed open to what I had in mind. In his email to me on 26 August 2016, he stated that he had received my request for the installation of a memorial garden and plaque for the many unmarked graves at Wilberforce Cemetery and in the Wesleyan Section.[1]

He mentioned that the Wilberforce Cemetery Conservation Management Plan did not allow for the development of a memorial garden within the site, but it did recognise that \ the establishment of a memorial garden could recognise the existence of unmarked burials in this area. He went on to say that Hawkesbury Council had bush regeneration contractors undertaking maintenance within the former Wesleyan Section, removing weeds and maintaining the native vegetation. To proceed with the development of a memorial garden in this section, he explained, Council would need to see a proposed design, details of the materials to be used, and an outline of the plant species to be included, which needed to be consistent with the area's native vegetation. Council would supply a list of suitable plant species. He attached a copy of signage already in place identifying the importance of the cemetery and the possibility of unmarked graves in the area, however that signage did not mention the names of at least 475 unmarked that were identified in the Conservation Management Plan.

"Wow," I thought to myself. "We have possibly more than 500 unmarked graves and souls wishing to be remembered here. We have work to do." No wonder I had so many souls trying to reach me to be recognised and acknowledged.

He completed his email by saying that the project would need to be reported to Council, given the significance of the site, showing his willingness to assist further in relation to design and location. He suggested the possibility of meeting on site to discuss it all further. Finally, it seemed things were moving forward. After a few emails back and forth, we had a meeting booked for 7 of September 2016, to stand on country and get a feel for what might be possible. I arrived at the Wesleyan Section that morning to meet a warm man who was genuinely interested in the project and open to helping me as much as he could. However, it seemed there would be quite a lot of the inevitable red tape that is generally expected in these types of projects.

We talked and walked along the tree-lined pathway that led to the circular area in the middle of the block, and he gave me ideas about what could be possible, while informing me of what was already happening on the land. This included radar scans that had been completed to determine whether there were graves in the Wesleyan section or not. Because of the number of trees, their roots made it difficult to tell if there were any burials on this site, though it was considered highly likely. In the early days of the colony, it was quite common for people who weren't baptised or otherwise unable to be buried in consecrated ground, to be buried outside the boundary of the church ground. So, there was a huge chance that some outsiders of the time were buried there. And they probably included Aboriginal people.

As we arrived in the centre of the circle at the end of the tree-lined path, he asked me what I was thinking of doing. I said, "I am thinking of a sandstone circle. Something like Stone Henge. A co-creation, not just a monument, but a living, nature temple of peace." He looked at me, a little puzzled.

"Really?" he said

"Yes, I feel we need to make a stone circle here."

A little overwhelmed by that option, he walked along the path, back to the road, discussing what would be needed to continue the journey to get something done. As we neared the entrance, he turned to me and asked,

"What was the name of your ancestor again?"

"Richard Shrimpton," I said. "Why do you ask?"

"Angela, I have only just been transferred to the Hawkesbury. Do you know what I have been doing the last couple of years?"

Of course, I had no idea.

"I have spent the last few years in Ryde and Epping working on the Historical Richard Shrimpton Creek Walk. And so, are you telling me now that Richard Shrimpton's great, great, great, great granddaughter is asking me to create this sacred site?"

I was quite stunned, but I opened my mouth and said, "Yes, it seems Richard is asking you, through me," I replied.

Within a split second I could see all the red tape that may have existed in his mind falling away, and his energy shifted to a commitment to help me fulfil the project. Even he couldn't believe the synchronicity of this situation. It was the next confirmation that we were indeed on track and should trust in what we were doing. We laughed about this incredible connection and began to make our way to our cars.

"One last thing, Angela, you need to connect with an Elder about this; it is really important. None of this can be done without their approval and consent. Talk soon. Oh! And it's Crown Land, so we will need into look what that means, and what we can do on Crown land."

"By the way," I called back. "Why did you finally get back to me?"

"The squeakiest wheel gets the oil Angela," he said as he disappeared into his car and drove off.

I sat in awe on the drive home, at how this was unfolding. The connection from the councillor to the Richard Shrimpton Creek Walk, that was dedicated to the memory of my ancestor.

I wondered, "How hard can it be to connect with an Elder?" As usual, God had my back. You can connect with many people, but finding those who will trust, love and stand with you on your journey is a different thing. Lucky for me, magic like that just seems to happen. I took the usual actions - emailing, calling, and asking others if they knew anyone who could help with this project. We must take action, we must do the next right thing we can do, and then when we have exhausted our options, let go and wait.

The next step, or any step in this journey was never generated by me, it was always and only ever handed to me by God as a mystical, synchronistic moment in time that I would never have imagined. I have had to learn to trust and act on the internal prompting and intuition that guides us all. When the student is ready, the teacher arrives, and he did. What was the next right thing? Well, there were two steps; to connect with an Elder most importantly, and secondly, I needed to write to the Queen. I realised that there was one essential aspect to this sacred site becoming sacred––the action that has never been taken by the Crown and its ancestors.

The healing must come from the top down. I must write to the Queen. Would she hear me? Would she even respond? And what could I say?

9

THE TEACHER APPEARS

"A teacher affects eternity; he can never tell where his influence stops."

- HENRY ADAMS

After the meeting, I got on with my week, and was asked to present at a raffle for a friend. Grace called me because, in her words, "you're good with a microphone, Ange, do you think you could come and give me a hand?"

Grace had put together a day to support elderly marginalised people in our area, pampering them with a lovely lunch, activities, and a lucky door raffle run by yours truly. I was busy, but committed to supporting Grace, especially because she had been so brave in her life, transforming ways of being that even she thought impossible. At the end of this event, Grace grabbed my arm and said, "Wait, there is someone I would love for you to meet."

She took me to see a man who was wearing a fabulous Akubra hat. The red, black and yellow band around its peak sported the words Proud & Deadly. It was literally a sliding door moment, where I could have left and been in my car and gone, rather than her introducing me. But Grace played her part in the ever growing and complex puzzle that was building.

"Uncle I would like you to meet Angela," she said, directing me to sit down. I was dumfounded, shocked at who I was standing in front of, somewhat like a stunned mullet. I thought to myself, why wouldn't there be an elder standing in front of me only days after I have been told I need to connect with one. And Uncle I quickly learned, was special. He was none other than Uncle Greg Simms, of the ancestral lineage of Gundungurra (water lizard people) of the Blue Mountains and Gadigal (whale people) people of the Dharug nation. Uncle Greg is one of Australia's foremost Elders and activists for reconciliation. I told him as much of the story as I could in the time we had, explaining that my next step was to connect with an Elder, and wham there he was.[1] He sat ever so quietly, listening and smiling, while I waited for some pearl of wisdom from him.

All he said was, "Hey bub, can you give me a lift home?"

In a little less than two days of realising what the next step was, I was introduced to one of the most kind and wise men I had ever met, and he happened to be one of Australia's foremost Elders. Everything felt surreal as I drove down the road, intermittently looking to my left to check whether I was dreaming, or if I really was driving down the road with one of Australia's most loved and respected Elders in my car? And yes, I was. Here he was. It felt like we were meeting again in this lifetime, just as we said we would before we came to Earth. It is hard not to imagine that we planned these meetings, and now we were just arriving on time.

As we pulled up at his home, he turned to me and said, "Hey bub, you reckon you could take me somewhere else I need to go?"

"No problem."

"I just need to change. I'll be back."

"Ok, sure," I said as he slowly got his walking stick, placed it on the ground, stood up and made his way inside. Turns out, while we were driving an email had arrived from Hawkesbury Council following up to see how I was going with connecting with an Elder. When Uncle Greg came back out, ready to go, he sat in the car and I showed him the email.

He grinned, "Hey, this fella doesn't know I am sitting right here, and we are going to go out there and check it out. Tell him we are going there to meet. Make a time and let me know. Ok, now let's go."

I sat there in awe. Within just two hours this beautiful man not only trusted me, but would stand with me, and come on country to talk about the project. I remember feeling surreal, feeling so blessed and humbled by life and all that it can bring when we commit to the journey, no matter how long or arduous. We arrived at his destination. He again took his walking stick, placed it on the ground and stepped out of the car to walk off.

As he did, he turned and said, "Hey, Bub, you're the one –" stopping mid-sentence. I was hanging off the last word.

"I'm the one. What?"

He smiled a cheeky grin, turned, and walked away.

"See ya, Bub, call me!"

And with that, he was gone.

Building bridges between our people. He brought me to meet other Elders in our area.

I emailed Council with a new proposal, to build a memorial, maybe even a stone circle, to acknowledge the unmarked names of those buried in Wilberforce Cemetery. The nature of this site changed as its purpose was to become a sacred site of love, peace, and forgiveness. An inspiration for the generations to come, of what this generation did, together. The unmarked names would end up on signage as a memorial, but the site wished to be more than a memorial or monument. It wished to be a sacred place. After a few attempts to follow-up, I received an email from a second representative of Hawkesbury Council. He thanked me for my previous correspondence regarding the possibility of creating a living memorial in the Wesleyan Section of Wilberforce Cemetery and apologised for the delay in reply. He acknowledged that I met with a Councillor in late 2016 with repeated follow-ups. He explained that staff had started action at my request, but unfortunately it progressed no further. He asked me to accept his apologies, and I replied that I hoped that they could now action my request fully. This was a positive email, one that came out of the blue. He moved on to say that Council had a Friends of Wilberforce Cemetery group that was very active. The group had helped to get the fence built around the cemetery and had established the contemplation area in the Wesleyan Section. He explained that the staff's aim was to arrange a meeting with me to discuss the proposal further.

He ended warmly by saying that he would be happy to facilitate such a meeting if I could give him some dates that would suit me to meet on the site. In the days before receiving the email, Uncle Greg had invited me to attend a meeting at Muru Mittigar, Rouse Hill. Uncle's intention was to give me a chance to connect with Elders and community regarding the project.

On the morning of the meeting, Uncle Greg asked me to come and collect him from his house, and on the way, we made a detour. He directed me to an address where I met a very special Elder, one of the oldest Elders in the area at 95 years of age at that time, now an incredible 99 years. Uncle Wes sat in the back of the car telling stories of times gone by, of his life, what happened to him all those years ago. It was a privilege to have this distinguished Elder in my car, and most movingly calling me Daughter.

I thought if I did nothing else, if this project came to naught, if I did not fulfil any other objectives, to sit with these beautiful and respected Elders and be called Daughter was one of the greatest, most valued achievements in this life. I could only bow my head with humility and love, as it was through the Elders' open hearts and unconditional love and forgiveness that this moment occurred.

I decided, once we were clear about what could be done on the land, we would go back to the wider generational community. This may seem like a slow process, but it really had to be treated with the utmost sensitivity and respect on both sides. When we truly commit to something of great significance and beauty, it can take a little time to complete.

10

AMAZING GRACE

"If it be a work of grace, it cannot fail."

– William Wilberforce

On 12 August 2018, a monumental realisation dropped while I prepared to write a letter to the Queen. As I sat bewildered at how to even begin, a question came to my mind. Wilberforce, who or what is that? As I searched, the name William Wilberforce popped out. It never really occurred to me to research the history behind the place. Wilberforce, or its namesake, is especially significant, considering the history of this country.

Eric Metaxas said it perfectly in his best-selling book *Amazing Grace: William Wilberforce and the Heroic Campaign to End Slavery*, "We often hear about people who need no introduction, but if there ever was someone who needed one, it is William Wilberforce. The irony is that we are talking about a man who changed the world, so if ever someone should not need an introduction, whose name and accomplishments should be on the lips of all humanity, it is William Wilberforce."[1]

I did not understand who he was, where he came from, and how he shaped the world. There is something mystical, something other-worldly about how this all unfolded despite my failings and lack of education on history. I find the guidance even more amazing because I did not understand how or where the synchronicities would connect and why. It has been through the unfolding of the journey that I can now see.

William Wilberforce was born 24 August 1759 and passed away 29 July 1833. He was a member of the English Parliament, a social reformer, and very influential in the abolition of slavery and the slave trade across the British Empire and Commonwealth, including and directly affecting Australia. The abolitionist Thomas Clarkson had a huge influence on Wilberforce. He and others were campaigning for the end of the slave trade on British ships that were carrying black slaves from Africa in terrible conditions to the West Indies as goods to be bought and sold. Clarkson inspired Wilberforce to lobby for the abolition of the slave trade, and for 18 years he regularly introduced anti-slave trade motions in parliament. In 1807 the slave trade was abolished, but this did not free the slaves who were already in slavery. It was not until 1833 that an act was passed to give freedom to all slaves in the British Empire.[2]

Midnight 31 August 1834, 800,000 slaves became free. It was more than a significant event in African or British history; it was one of the greatest events in the history of mankind.[3] When William Wilberforce died, he was buried in Westminster Abbey. Staring at the dozens of books written about him, I was moved to tears after realising the significance of the name of the land upon which we were working to create this vision of peace in Australia.

As I sat at my computer, I had a vivid experience, almost to the point of being able to imagine William standing beside me in his 18th Century regalia. I had finally connected with him as the namesake of this land, and someone who would, with his energy and love, assist us from beyond the veil to achieve our aim.

I realised that this really could be possible. We were gathering on both sides of the veil, and we were receiving experienced, powerful and determined support. With the help of the ancestors, ancients, guides and mentors, we really could be the ones to create something of significance, and hand this land back to the original owners as a symbol of our commitment to transformation and change. I was sobered by the vast amount of work to be done, but honoured to fulfil my small part of this amazing story.

For the longest time, ever since I truly understood the magnitude of devastation that happened due to the colonisation of this country, I had an unspoken distaste for my white skin. I had days when I looked around the world and thought about its history and wished I could peel my skin from my body and sit naked with my flesh, rather than own the colour of my skin, and the history it carried with it. I hoped that somewhere in my First or Second Fleet history there would be a blood connection to a First Nations person so I could feel less white. I hated my history. I found some pride in individuals and their achievements, but it paled compared to the overwhelming feeling that I couldn't be proud of my British roots. William Wilberforce changed this for me.

When my father passed away, he died without a Will. I'm not sure why he didn't complete this task. He was a paramedic, a switched on and intelligent man who kept impeccable notes and reports on every aspect of his life. Maybe it was fear; maybe he felt that if he signed a Will, it was signing his life away. We will never know for sure, but it left us with a monumental task to complete his estate.

Holding the role of administrator for his estate, I began the journey of understanding white man's law, its language and expressions. It annoyed me that Dad had left us in such a predicament, that we now had to fight the law to complete his life. We couldn't even pick up his mail as everything (rightly so) gets locked up to protect it.

My father's death instigated my initiation into white law, into the old language and means of correspondence that echoes with a British tone. I saw in myself a deep need to heal and accept myself as not only a white woman who has a biological connection to the British First, Second, and ongoing Fleets in Australia, but also a woman of Irish, Scottish, and Nordic ancestry. As a living ancestor it is my responsibility and honour to respond in whatever way I can, to mend the broken pieces of our relationships for the greater good of the future. It is a task to bless those who will enjoy this place hundreds and thousands of years from now. Just as we were not there when the colonists arrived in 1788, but inherited the waves of past suffering in our present, we can bequeath future generations with waves of peace and healing.

What fresh waves will we make, what storms will we calm? What choices will we make that will have us known as the generation who looked our past in the face and did what needed to be done?

We are all one; we came from the same place and will return there once again. But in this physical world we have biological ancestors that pass down information, learnings, ability, talents, and traumas on a cellular level from one generation to the next. There are messages in my genetics that go back to the people of old, the lands my ancestors came from, those that danced around Stonehenge or even helped to build it, who knows? But what I recognise is that it is time, rather than being ashamed of my British heritage, to find its greatest potential to remedy injuries, and make my ancestors proud. I came to see I had been rejecting my ancestors, so how could they speak to and through me? I was a closed vessel unwilling to unlock the jewels waiting in my blood. But Mary Davis Bishop, Richard Shrimpton and the ancestors had left crumbs along the way for me to connect the dots and find my path. My experiences seemed unrelated, and yet looking back I could see just how connected every step was. It was enough to make me wonder if I had any control at all.

I realised that I needed to be the very best version of myself, in this skin. I needed to love myself for who I am, for I am not my past, nor my ancestor's past; I am what I live up to and create in this world in every moment. I am my highest potential in the ever-present now, and I believe that by committing to the possibility of miracles, peace, healing, and love we can see the dawn of a new day, a unified future for our country.

Australia is now a land that has been woven into a thousand breathtaking colours of the world, and we must unite to celebrate our First Nations people and give back to them what they never ceded: their sovereignty. As we do this, we shall simultaneously set ourselves free from the self-imposed prison we live in subconsciously. The prison of our fear of the truth, of change, and of letting go. It brings to mind a teaching of Uncle Greg, who always completes his Welcome to Country by saying, "Don't you think the music would sound better using both the black and white keys?" He's right. It does.

So, as I prepared myself to write letters to the Queen, I felt William Wilberforce stand by my side. I could almost hear his voice saying, "for wisdom and strength and power of persuasion, may you surrender yourself to God, as to the event with perfect submission and ascribe to him all the praise if you succeed, and if you fail, say from the heart, Thy will be done." (Eric Metaxas. Amazing Grace. William Wilberforce)[4]

John Newton, the author of the world-famous song Amazing Grace, is one of the most incredible souls born to humanity. As a confidant, mentor and friend to Wilberforce, he encouraged William to pursue his gargantuan goal of abolishing slavery in Britain.When William found himself at a crossroads, his faith inspiring him to join the clergy, it was John who convinced him that he ought to walk both the political *and* spiritual paths, bringing spirituality to his vocation and purpose to his politics.[5]

It is my deep conviction that the ancestors walk among us, and like St Therese, wish to do their significant works from spirit, so we become their mortal hands and feet. You may ask why this chapter celebrates a white man. Some of you may wonder how this celebration is in alignment with seeking the return of sovereignty, treaty, peace, love and respect to our First Nations people. My aim is to provide balance to see that among us, no matter the colour of our skin, no matter where we come from or who we are, there are souls who will stand for humanity, peace, compassion and harmony between us all. Wilberforce died three days after he achieved his purpose to abolish slavery in the Commonwealth. As I learnt about this inspiring man, I felt proud of my lineage that came from the same place as such an enlightened and determined human.

A golden doorway opened with the abolishment of slavery, almost

190 years ago, that guided our British ancestors to a new way of thinking about humanity, and showed that it was possible to achieve the seemingly impossible. Imagining William Wilberforce standing beside me, I wrote my first letter to Queen Elizabeth II, all the while imagining Wilberforce's English accent, and with his help, the letter came forth.

Her Majesty the Queen
Buckingham Palace
LONDON
SW1A 1AA
August 2018

Your Majesty,

My name is Angela Mary Sciberras, and I am a direct descendant of First and Second Fleet convicts, Mary Davis Bishop and Richard Shrimpton, who travelled to Australia on the Lady Penrhyn and Scarborough, respectively. I am humbled to express the importance of the request I am to present to you. A divine calling on my life. This letter represents a calling that was born over 20 years ago, from the whisperings of what I believe to be the voices of time gone by. My ancestors travelled the fierce seas to arrive in Australia broken and ill-prepared for what lay ahead of them. That they survived their trips of inexplicable hardship and trial is an extraordinary feat.

I sincerely and formally request the support and attendance of Your Majesty the Queen or a representative of the Crown, at a Sacred Ceremony that I humbly believe will surpass all conducted or taken part in by the Crown or its lineage since the time of seeding the foundations of this modern nation. When I consider the magnitude of the subject that I bring to your attention I am confronted and overcome by the responsibility it lays bare for us all. I am completing what I consider the greatest responsibility of my lifetime, to apologise, recognise, and seek reconciliation with the Aboriginal people of Australia. To stand upon Dharug land, now serendipitously named after one of Britain's most beloved subjects, William Wilberforce, who in his lifetime inspired more men and women than any other in the service of humanity and equality. I feel God / Conscience has set before me Three Great Objects:

1. The completion of a Sandstone Circle: (in the Wesleyan Section of the Wilberforce Cemetery) at Wilberforce NSW, Australia. This will be a joint creation between the First Nations people and settler descendants for recognition and reconciliation of the Traditional Owners of this country. This small parcel of land is marked 'Crown Land.' The proposed Stone Circle will also stand as an act of grace in naming all unmarked graves in this significant cemetery, including that of my ancestor Richard Shrimpton. Wilberforce Cemetery is of great national significance with rich and rare evidence of Australia's earliest ex-convict pioneer society. Having been given permission by Hawkesbury Council, to create a memorial, I feel it weighs heavily on my mind and heart, to create a much deeper act of significance. I hope that you can see the power we have in our hands to create something together as Crown, First Nations, and First Settler descendants. I have witnessed in the early stages of the development of this project, the coming together and embracing of direct lines of both First Nations and Settler descendants, and it is beyond moving. How extraordinarily powerful an act we could partake in, to stand on land named after the greatest reformer of all time, William Wilberforce, the hero for humanity, at a ceremony, along with First Nations and settler descendants, heart to heart, making the past right, and beginning a new narrative for history to tell. It's time for the land to heal, along with its people, releasing us all, including the Crown, from the bonds and pain of the past. Descendants of those directly involved, standing in unity for the sake of peace for our future generations.

2. The Action of Greater Significance I seek is to hand this 'Crown Land' now named The Wesleyan Section, back to the Traditional Owners, with your seal of approval and support, where henceforth will stand a memorial and sacred place of remembrance, reconciliation, and unity. The days of creating monuments and gardens in the name of peace, with the belief that such a token act be enough to show sincerity, are over. It is time for a powerful act, from one descendant to another. A powerful symbol of the now genuine nature of our plan to reconcile our past for a peaceful, prosperous future for all Australians.

3. I seek a heartfelt apology and acknowledgement from the Crown, for misdeeds and injustices suffered by both settlers and First Nations people of Australia. I humbly request a letter and expression of the Crown's support of the reconciliation between our people, and the extension of a vision of a prosperous path ahead. I humbly request within this historical document the expression of profound regret and apology for lives lost because of any hostilities resulting from its invasion. This would be a moral and ethical act, an act of good conscience and a demonstration of respect for all humanity, with the overall goal of restoring dignity and harmony, to love people and seek to do good. I need not remind you, though I find it fitting to bring to your attention, of this most victorious of days in the history of Britain, humanity and the world.

"The evening of 23 February 1807 was unforgettable. In the British House of Commons Parliamentary debate had started on the second reading of a bill calling for the abolition of the British slave trade. For twenty years similar bills were introduced, only to go down to defeat. But this night would be different. As the debate began one Member of Parliament, after another rose to praise the man who would refuse to accept defeat in his efforts to secure the abolition of the slave trade. The scene was electric. Before one member had finished speaking, others jumped to their feet, wishing to add their voices to the overwhelming

tide of support for Wilberforce's bill. Wilberforce sat in his place, head bowed, and wept; tears of joy streamed down his face. There upon the commons voted on an overwhelming majority to abolish the British slave trade."
- Kevin Belmont [6]

The irony is that my ancestor, Richard Shrimpton, a convict from the Second Fleet, now lies buried in the Dharug soil named after this man. No one has done more than Wilberforce to inspire, free, and serve humanity and God, a British commoner, in whom my ancestral identity can find much pride. Pride I must admit was found wanting prior to this revelation, yet is now restored in the enormity of his contribution – a contribution that it seems I am charged to uphold. This vision existed before my knowledge of the grandeur of Wilberforce, noting the somewhat mysterious serendipity of our missions aligned over 200 years, standing for the equality of all men and unity.

Akin to words from Wilberforce's most famous "Abolition Speech" on May 12, 1789, House of Commons, London; "When these reflections press upon my mind, it is impossible for me not to feel both terrified and concerned at my inadequacy to such a task." It is the encouragement from my fellow men and women, many other descendants, and Indigenous leaders, which has strengthened my conviction and increased my faith. To be of honest expression, I must sincerely admit that it is only in recent days that I can say with some amount of shame, that I realise the great significance of the name "Wilberforce" in the history of Great Britain and our entire world.

I humbly suggest what a historical feat of our generation it would be to extend the hands of time, and forward such a powerful act of peace, inspiring not only our nation, but the world, particularly when humanity most urgently needs inspiration and reconnection, with the aim of genuine restoration of faith in the relevance of Queen and Country, The Crown, our Australian Government and Leadership.

Luke 12:48 in the King James Bible reminds us: *"For unto whomsoever much is given, of him shall be much required."* Many today argue that there is little relevance of Royalty in our modern society of Australia. I disagree with that statement and believe that what I suggest in this letter could put an end to that argument. Your Highness, in the name of one so extraordinary as William Wilberforce, you could create a thread of hope and outward expression of the highest use of worldly power and fame. I know that the power to which you answer is divine, and therefore I see this act as an expression of your divinity. I believe you have the people of the world at heart. Like Wilberforce, I determine to forget all of my other fears and march forward with a firmer step with a full assurance that my cause will bear me out, and that I shall be able to justify upon the clearest principles, every resolution in my hand; the avowed end of which is the heartfelt apology given from the Crown itself to the Indigenous people of Australia for the past injustices they have endured. I mean not to accuse anyone, but to take the shame upon myself in common with the whole Crown, Parliament of Great Britain and Australia, for them having suffered this horrid past. It is time for truth and treaty.

An apology is a peace offering, and an act of humility and humanity. The value of an apology for the people who receive it can be immeasurable in its ripple effect of healing and peace. For a victim, we often consider the apology to be the key that will unlock the door to healing. It propels us onto a pathway of restoring the damaged relationship, by expressing the regret for causing someone to suffer, and an attempt to diminish their pain. Allow a unique opportunity for us to stand upon the shoulders of one of the greatest men of all time, a British subject no less. Wilberforce stood for socially controversial legislation and campaigned for justice for all, racial equality and concern for the poor in heart. Let us heed his call, even from the grave, passing note and acknowledging that this stand is no less controversial than that which Wilberforce worked his entire life to complete.

As an example of what is possible, I bring your attention to Her Majesty's apology to the Indigenous Maori people of New Zealand in 1995. I would humbly request a similar act taken by the Crown to put a signature to an abject apology to Aboriginal Australia to express profound regret and apologies for losing lives because of the hostilities arising from its invasion and for the devastation of property and culture that resulted. I wish not to offend Her Majesty, being aware and fully comprehending that while the document will be in the name of the Crown, it will not be a personal apology, but recognise the Royal signature being highly significant to our nation, and the Indigenous of Australia.

I will not, therefore, condemn Crown and Great Britain, I will allow it, nay, I will believe it to be filled with men and women of humanity. Like Wilberforce, I will therefore believe that if it were not for the enormous magnitude and extent of the evil that can often distract us from what happened here, we might have clarity and therefore compassion regarding our history. I truly believe that our ancestors would never have persisted in this course of action if we had known the scars that would be left upon the hearts and minds of the Aboriginal people.

I humbly suggest that the Crown seeks to make this a reality to reveal its great strength, relevance, and commitment to the wellbeing of its people past and present. We look to you for such wisdom that surpasses all others, in following the law of "love your neighbour as yourself."

I believe that a heartfelt apology from the Crown, and the return of this Crown Land to the First Nations people is a beautiful, firm and tangible act of grace that is urgently needed. The Bible tells us we should love others as we love ourselves; then we need to go out and do just that. And we are all bound to serve and follow "common law, to love thy neighbour as ourselves, and love your Lord God with all your heart and all your mind." In following these laws, to me the most obvious and compassionate action is clear and required.

We are at a fork in the road in history that beseeches us to choose the path it requires – duty and principle – even if it means hardship and struggle. It was Wilberforce's belief, along with mine, that before God, our deepest obligation is to follow the dictates of our conscience. This binding commitment was beautifully expressed in a letter Wilberforce wrote concerning the Abolition of the Slave Trade in 1793.

"With every question of political expediency, there appears to me room for

the consideration of times and seasons. At one period under one set of circum-
stances it may be proper to push, at another under other circumstances to with-
hold our efforts. But in the present instance where the actual commission of
guilt is in question a man who fears God is not at liberty, to persuade then
that I shall never make this grand cause the sport of caprice, or sacrifice it to
motives of personal convenience, or personal feeling. We are at such a time in
our nation's history where we are being called to put aside all motives and per-
sonal convenience to make the wrongs right and stand for justice, served in the
name of love and equality. It is time for the treaty and actions that result from
its creation. True liberty is a plant of celestial growth and none can perceive its
beauties but those who have employed the nobler faculties of the human soul in
completing the divine goodness from what it springs. I hope the day will arrive
when all mankind will enjoy its blessings."[7]

May we, like John Newton, all be subject to amazing grace, even after close to 200 years since the miracle Wilberforce made manifest. Let
the policy be what it might, let the consequences be what they may.
I, from this time, am determined that I will never rest until I put the
wrongs of my own ancestors right, live to see a formal and sincere apology from the Crown, and ultimately the miraculous creation of a formal treaty between the Crown, our Australian Government, and the
First Nations people of this land. This letter comes with the highest of
regard, honour and respect. I send my deep gratitude for your divine
example of leadership and strength; it is of immeasurable wealth to our
world.

Your Majesty's humble servant,

Angela Mary Sciberras

Reply: 8th November 2018

Dear Mrs Sciberras,

The Queen has asked me to thank you for your recent letter in which you wished to tell Her Majesty about the community project you are initiating. Perhaps I might explain, however, that this is not a matter in which the Queen would intervene. As a constitutional Sovereign, Her Majesty acts through her personal representative, the Governor General, on the advice of her Australian Ministers and therefore, it is to them that your appeal should be directed. Nevertheless, it was most thoughtful of you to write as you did.

Yours Sincerely,
Miss Jennie Vine
Deputy Correspondence Co-ordinator

My Response:
Miss Jennie Vine MVO
Deputy Correspondence Coordinator
Her Majesty the Queen
Buckingham Palace LONDON
SW1A 1AA

Your Majesty,

My name is Angela Sciberras and I wrote a letter to you a few weeks ago. I thank you for receiving it. I was happy to receive your letter dated 8 November 2018. I am deeply privileged and grateful that you took the time to read my letter and give me a response that was encouraging and sincere. Thank you.

On Her Majesty's advice I have sent my appeal again, for the second time to our Governor General, Sir Peter Cosgrove, to request his assistance to act within his highest powers and principles to request this support in the creation of this miracle in peacemaking. Considering that, through Common Law, the highest value upon which our law and Constitution rests is to 'Love thy Neighbour,' I look forward to his swift response in alignment with this law we all might abide by.

I have sent my letters, along with your response, to our Prime Minister, and also representative of Aboriginal Issues and Affairs and Special Envoy. That I am given opportunity to have my heart and mind heard, and the voices of the past be given the right of peace of mind and right action is a profound privilege, I thank you. I believe Her Majesty could have written to me and given me no direction as to how to complete what I believe is my destiny, but instead I was gifted with a path with dignity and respect to have her freely act within the constitution, in a way that she can, to have this great act in the name of our First Nations, in the name of my ancestors, the name of the Crown, and in the name of the hero of humanity, William Wilberforce.

It would be an honour to personally collect from Buckingham Palace "The Queen's Letter," and to hence transport this precious work of paper, pen, power, peace, and privilege to the people of this Nation of Australia. Such a simple act. Mere paper. Ink and love in action. I beg your pardon and thank you for at minimum hearing my request, that even in the asking, not knowing whether it can indeed be done, it is magnificent and beautiful. To remind you.

I feel God / Conscience has set before me Three Great Objects:

1. The completion of a Sandstone Circle in the Wesleyan Section of the Wilberforce Cemetery, at Wilberforce, NSW, Australia. This will be a joint creation between the First Nations people and convict ancestry for the purpose of recognition and reconciliation of the Traditional Owners of this country and our ancestors.

2. The Action of Greater Significance I seek is to hand this Dharug land, now labelled Crown Land and named the Wesleyan Section, back to the Traditional Owners, with your seal of approval and full support, where henceforth will stand a memorial and sacred place of remembrance, reconciliation, and unity. The days of creating monuments and gardens in the name of peace, with the belief that such a token act be enough to show sincerity are over.

3. I seek a heartfelt apology and acknowledgement from the Crown; I humbly request a letter and expression of the Crown's support of the reconciliation between our people, and the extension of a vision of a prosperous path ahead. I humbly request within this historical document the expression of profound regret and apology. The honouring of the Indigenous people of this land and regret for the suffering and loss of First Nations people. This, a moral and ethical act, an act of good conscience and demonstration of respect for all humanity, with the overall goal of restoring dignity, sovereignty and harmony. I believe in the supreme love and power you have sworn to, in what it has taken to be a great Monarch, and in what God entrusted

in you all those years ago. I am humbled by who you have the opportunity to be in the world, in gratitude.

Humbly,

Angela Sciberras

I I

THE UNSPOKEN
AGREEMENT

"The history of thousands of Aborigines was determined, in part, as a result of the Myall Creek massacre. A new unwritten law emerged, death by stealth."

- BRUCE ELDER

There are moments in time that act as lynch pins, holding our position, even when we wish we could change it. Why? To survive. Because we are afraid. Because of the beliefs that change the way we see ourselves. The pain that encourages us to shut down and build walls around us, and the agreements we make, whether spoken or unspoken affect us as individuals, and even the unfolding of the history of an entire nation.

We have a profound responsibility when writing and telling stories. History spoken and passed down through generations can become binding, preventing us from growing, having compassion, understanding and ultimately being set free from the bonds of old mental constructs and ideologies. Like a blind spot, we are often unaware of the mental prisons designed to control and keep one small. The truth however can be diamond like, with many facets of perception. The diamond in its fullness, revealing formerly unseen sides, can be both elevating and devastating all at once.

Bruce Elder's book Blood on the Wattle triggered an endless flood of tears, flowing from the shock of how gruesome many of the events in our Australian history were. To prevent the theft of flour, tea or food of any kind, they placed large metal traps in the fields. These mantraps were so powerful, no single person could pull them apart. Aboriginals were hung from branches and decapitated, their heads placed in storerooms to keep other potential thieves at bay. Loaves of damper laced with arsenic were provided as payment for jobs completed, corpses were skinned and filled with grass; heads were placed on fence posts around properties as a warning for anyone thinking of passing through the settlers' newly acquired land.

Maybe I had gleaned a sense of relief at the thought the responsibility of Australia's early bloody history lay with the Crown only. Deep down, surely, I knew that wasn't true, and facing the details of the decimation, I could no longer hold tight to that internal myth. Moulded and shaped by an elite and often unseen hand, and a system of control for many generations, no matter our colour, creed, or country, all races and peoples have perpetrated, or been the victims of slavery, brutal treatment, and genocide of all kinds. This is ultimately a trait we as human beings share; one I hope we are ready to overcome and evolve out of.

If we continue to project the blame and responsibility to an outside force, we cannot restore our own power and freedom. The power truly is in our hands. To hold a new hope that as humans we may finally rise together, throwing down the chains of the past to build a new world on the foundations of love, compassion, peace and equality. In saying that, seeing the past for all it was, and all it wasn't is part of the path of healing, the past a powerful teacher, providing the lessons why we must work together to abandon all notions of returning to it. Myall Creek is one such teacher.

On 5 of June 1838, on Henry Dangar's Myall Creek Station, where 40 Kwiambal Aborigines lived in harmony with the settlers and stockmen, a brutal massacre occurred. Terrified men, women and children, along with babies wrapped in possum coats, were tied up with rope and led out of sight into the frosty night air. The next day brought an unbearable truth. Piles of half-burned bodies, the ground soaked with blood. Inconceivably, the men that had committed the murders had dismembered the bodies, that desecration making it impossible to accurately count the number of dead. Governor Gipps saw the events of this massacre as an opportunity to reassert British law on the frontier and ordered an investigation with a view to prosecution.[1]

Sufficient evidence was gathered to lay charges. The accused Charles Kilmeister, John Russell, George Palliser, John Johnstone, Edward Ned Foley, Charles Toulouse, James Hawkins, John Blake, Charles 'Jem' Lamb, James Perry and James Oates. The twelfth man, and only free settler among the perpetrators, John Fleming, fled and evaded capture, but I would come across his name again, later in my journey. Under British law, both blacks and whites were equal. But such was the public outrage to the arrests, that groups formed to defend the prisoners. On 15 November 1838, at the Supreme Court in Sydney the case was summed up as a grievous offence. But despite the considerable evidence put forth, the jury took a mere 15 minutes to pronounce all 11 men not guilty. The crowd in the court burst into loud applause. Frontier law had overwhelmed British justice, though not for long it seemed, as the 11 men were kept in custody to be retried for the crime, using the same evidence.[2]

The retrial officially began on 29 November, in the shadow of newspapers calling for the release of the prisoners, and reviling the intentions of Governor Gipps for justice. Only seven of the original 11 men, Kilmeister, Russell, Foley, Oats, Johnstone, Parry and Hawkins, were charged with the murders at the second trail. Blake, Toulouse, Palliser and Lamb were to be retried separately, but that never occurred. The seven who were retried were found guilty and on the 7th of December were sentenced to death by hanging. They had confessed to the slayings but claimed in their defence that killing Aboriginals was such a common frontier sport, they had not realised it was illegal.[3]

As Bruce Elder writes, in Blood on the Wattle, the executions, which took place on 18 December 1838, shocked the settlement - the importance of a moment in time, and what people would make it mean would now come into play. The Crown had hoped that the trial and its outcome would send a warning to not kill Aboriginals. Instead it seems the message received by squatters and frontiersman was, 'If you kill Aboriginals, don't, under any circumstance, let the authorities know. 'The result of the trial and the executions was that nearly all future massacres in New South Wales went unrecorded, thus, Elder suggests, "the history of thousands of Aboriginals was determined, in part, because of the Myall Creek massacre. A new, unwritten law emerged: death by stealth."[4]

While this above book does not intend to apportion blame, I am concerned with acknowledging and understanding what happened, and more than that, what meaning was taken from what happened. I see that the universal, human shared experience of greed and thirst for power created actions and behaviour that, ultimately had a huge cost for the future of this country and all who inhabit it.

Myall Creek was a turning point. A silent, unconscious agreement that still exists within the fabric of our modern society for many, an agreement I feel we are transforming with every day that passes.

12

ONEMOBDREAMING

"The Elders taught by example that everything was sacred and that nature whispers to those who seek her council."

— SCOTT ALEXANDER KING

One of my first gifts as a baby was a pin: two little blue swallows with yellow cheeks, connected together by a chain. This pin was one of my most cherished items. I kept them with me in many times of challenge and fear, like two little messengers that would keep me safe. I always had a special relationship with swallows, they seemed to arrive in sacred moments, darting through the air like tiny rockets with wings.

I noticed them arrive at times I was in the cemetery visiting my ancestors, and even times when sitting alone in nature and thinking of someone who had long passed away. Souls of the dearly departed is what I would think to myself, the gift of a little magic, and a reminder that we are never alone.

Swallows were so revered in ancient Greece, as symbols of the goddess of Love, Aphrodite, that it was sacrilegious to kill a swallow or rob its nest. They were celebrated as symbols of rebirth, resurrection and new life. Associated with heaven, sent to earth as angelic comforts, the ancient Romans believed they were the souls of children who would visit their home and family. They were thought to protect and inspire the lives of people during spring, summer, and winter, returning to heaven in the autumn. Darting through the air, they symbolically stir up and agitate negativity, stagnation and any trace of heavy energy hiding in the shadows. Their anchor-like tails harness, ground and surrender to the universe. Swallow dreaming works in much the same way as a spiritual guide, leading us to realise our potential and purpose. [1]

For me, swallows have shown up at some of the most pivotal moments in my life, including in 2011, after I had my own near-death experience, as a result of an ectopic pregnancy. By the time the hospital worked out what was going on I had all but bled out internally, with no idea that I was living on borrowed time. Wheeled in to have what should have been a textbook ectopic surgery, over five hours later I was wheeled out to a worried husband, and learnt that I had been lucky to survive the ordeal. The embryo had attached to my ovary, and the ovary had burst. So, I lost both an ovary and our child of ten weeks that day.

My first memory of this experience was waking up to the voice of Dr Ganesh (immediately knowing I would be okay). Dr Ganesh said in a thick accent, "you are very lucky, all things considered, you should be dead." This was a devastating, and life changing moment. It left me unwell for a year or so. With the loss of the ovary, the trauma of the pain and extensive blood loss, I was left feeling like I had only one foot in this world for years to follow. It was like a part of me died that day, and the person left now felt different, and saw the world differently. It took a long time to recover, but it was music, sound and my experience seeing my favourite human and musician of all time, Prince, live on stage that healed my heart. By the time I left the stadium, I was alive again, I could feel again, and wanted to live for the first time in over a year. I noticed myself walking with swagger, my funk had returned.

From that time on I was grateful to Prince as someone who embodied the love-filled and powerful genius that created music with the ability to heal. Whenever I felt down, I would put on his music and all would be OK. Over time I built a strong connection and respect for him as a person and artist. When he passed away on 21 April 2016, I remember waking up at 6am, feeling like I needed to check my phone. The first thing that popped up was the news that Prince was dead. The shock, the pain, the sadness and disbelief was overwhelming. As I look back now it's almost like he knew he was about to go. His last series of performances found him coming full circle to the one instrument that seemed to trigger him, because it was his father's. I can't say for sure, but it seemed to me that Prince longed, and subconsciously strove through all of his endeavours and achievements, to be as good as his father.

In 2012, when I saw him on stage, Prince told the crowd that he looked forward to returning to Sydney one day to perform at the Opera House, and he did. My cousin, sister-in-law and I attended one of his last performances at the Sydney Opera House in 2016, just him and the piano on stage. At the end of the show I purchased a tee shirt depicting the 13-moon cycle, a piano, and his face in a misty form above. How did we not see it? When I look at this image now it is almost like he knew he had come full circle and his journey was about to end. But here it was, he was gone.

In the days following I made a pact with myself that I would buy a guitar and start playing his music. The amazing thing is that only 24 hours later we were walking in an area we rarely frequent. I passed a hock shop, and something made me look harder. I had never walked into the shop before, but as I walked to the back, there, in all its glory was The Cloud, hanging on the wall. I stood there with my mouth open. The Cloud was the white guitar that Prince played in the movie Purple Rain, some say the most iconic instrument in history. And here it was on the wall? Needless to say, I felt this synchronicity was one of my most precious, and the Cloud now hangs in an ornate white, gold, and purple suede frame, my most prized and holy possession. Prince's Cloud Guitar. What is even more amazing is that in the movie Purple Rain, Apollonia sees Prince looking at the Cloud in the window of a shop. She ended up buying it for him as a gift.

Was this a gift from Prince to me? I'd like to think so, thousands would disagree. But the chances I would find The Cloud in a shop in Western Sydney, a day after promising myself I would buy a guitar and start playing his music have to be a million to one. I didn't imagine for a second that I could ever find The Cloud. But there it was. And to boot I got it for a steal because the owner of the hock shop thought it was Pink's guitar. Let's just say I had to hold back from immediately slapping that man's face when those sacrilegious words came out of his mouth. I could hear Prince's iconic voice say "Damn man! I will pretend I didn't hear that."

Back to the swallows ... months before I saw Prince in 2012, not long after I had my near-death experience, I left the house to go and take a slow walk along the river at Richmond. I was walking along with my two dogs Ruby and Archie, when all of a sudden, the most extraordinary thing occurred. What looked like at least a thousand swallows darted and flew towards me. I was actually afraid they would hit me, but instead they all began flying in a circle around me, so tight I closed my eyes afraid of ending up with a swallow in the eye! They circled faster and faster and it became like a tornado of swallows flying around me. I stood there overwhelmed, and as quickly as they came, they disappeared into the blue sky. I stood there, actually feeling a lot better, and truly amazed at what had just taken place.

Few would believe such a thing, but it happened. From then on, I became acutely aware of the presence of swallows, when they were around me, becoming strong signs of spirit and my connection to the underworld. Looking back, I now believe my near-death experience had to happen for me to truly begin to connect to the ancestors and spirits on the other side. Almost like I had to cheat death to be able to embody both life and death in one. Some have called me a death walker because of my work with the dying, and they may be right, I don't really know. Many years later the swallows would return in a powerful way, when I was guided by the many afore-mentioned signs and symbols to Uluru.

The day we went to see the rock itself, it was flooding. There was so much water around Uluru that we had to take off our shoes and roll up our pants to walk around it in knee deep water. You couldn't hear yourself think with the sound of the frogs calling in the desert. It was surreal. All of a sudden, from inside Uluru, came thousands of swallows. They poured out over us, and began to circle, much like they did after I had almost died years before. I stood there, my two little blue swallows' pin in hand. They circled us for quite some time as tears flowed down my face, I could almost hear the ancestors say "It's okay, you will be okay, all will be okay." It was one of the most memorable moments of my life.

One of the main reasons I had been led there was to meet a friend and brother named Uncle Allan. Uncle Allan is the CEO, and Founder of an emerging company named Garlugun Girrwaa Yuludarla – Onemobdreaming. Uncle Allan would end up being an integral part of the journey ahead as the bridge, or as a Boundary Rider. Uncle Allan has both Indigenous (Gumbangiiyarr / Worimi) and Non-Indigenous (Irish / European) ancestry, and is therefore a bridge between two worlds. Uncle Allan became someone I could go to with questions and frustrations, and a loyal friend who believes in me, my journey, and this story.

Onemobdreaming (Garlugun Girrwaa Yuludarla) is the dreaming of all people uniting back together upon country in the proper way. When I asked Uncle Allan what he meant by proper way he said, "Proper way is living by the universal laws passed down by our ancestors of how to live on mother earth, together in harmony with all things. They may be old ways, but we can work together to bring old ways to new days. To bring unity back into the word community.

Proper way is looking at how we consume, the effects of our ways on mother earth within our family and global community. How our actions are affecting one another and our ability to live peacefully, in harmony on the mother. The earth is our mother, and we are her family. Proper way is the way of the heart, working/living with our mother and knowing that all things are connected."

"We are only here as custodians to look after our mother, to grow and become better humans, better people within the family and community of our world. Onemobdreaming is my dreaming (journey), the job I came here to do, as shown and taught to me by a senior Elder (whom I had the honour to call Father) and the many loving, guiding Aunties and Uncles along the way of my continual learning, my remembering. Father and a dearly loved Uncle shared a dreaming story that we were created as one people on the earth, and over time we have split, creating much diversity across the planet over many years. It is part of this dreaming, that it is time to unite once again as one people, one people unified within the diversity of our world. We can be one, enjoying, respecting, and walking together for a better future for the little ones to come."

"We endeavour to create a better way of being, a better way of being within ourselves and the world, it's not about being perfect, but being respectful. Working together as one, whilst respecting and celebrating our differences as unity in diversity. Working within the arts, education, health, culture and reconciliation. Envy knows no colour, greed knows no colour, hatred knows no colour, ego knows no colour; they are all human attributes. But so is love, so is sharing, so is compassion. Equally, respect and understanding are human attributes."

Uncle Allan says, "The past must be told, taught and shared, truthfully and honestly. It must be understood so that we can stand together for it to never happen again. And it is important to say that there are many good bits to this story. Not all people, all settlers or colonisers who came to this country were bad people. There were some who loved, cared for, and protected Aboriginal people. There were kind and compassionate settlers who did treat the people proper way, and for that we are grateful and honour and respect those people. But we still need to talk about the sadness, the poisonings, the hangings and the massacres, and all that has brought us to now. That all must be spoken about before we can move forward. We must also look at the injustices happening to the Aboriginal people today, the stolen generation has not stopped, it has just taken a new form."

"Of course the history must be spoken about so that we may show deep respect to those who were crushed by it, it must be spoken about so that we may be able to truly move forward and return dignity to the people who once had so much respect and love for one another and the mother. People who have lived on country for more than 60,000 years as loving custodians, and children of the mother. It is time to restore the Indigenous people to an equal ground and place within Australian society, along with all members of the world family."[2]

It was perfect that the Queen had not responded to my second letter, nor had the Governor General. I realised that this path was one we needed to walk together. If the letter and stone circle were to become a reality, if peace in this country or at least its beginnings were to become a reality, we needed to do it together, as one mob, dreaming the new reality as one.

13

THE TWO-SIDED COIN

"We cannot walk forward and leave others behind because that is not proper way. We all walk together, that can be the ONLY WAY."

- UNCLE ALLAN PHILLIPS

On 8 February 2018, I made my way out to the Wesleyan Section with a group of supporters, to connect, meditate and prepare for what would take place the next day. The coming together of the descendants of those buried in the Wilberforce Cemetery, Aboriginal Elders Uncle Greg and Uncle Allan, representatives of the Hawkesbury Council, and a few interested friends who supported the project.

As we travelled, Uncle Allan and I spoke about the concept of being a two-sided coin. Ultimately, we are one, but each have our own side of life. We talked at length about this as we drove to the entrance of the cemetery to park. It was a warm day, very little breeze, and yet there was still a lone Hawk in the sky, our usual sign of the significance of the day and time.

We decided to take a walk through the cemetery; Allan wished to connect to the old people and the land. We meandered through the old, hand-carved headstones, solid demonstrations of the mastery of the 17th and 18th century stonemasons. Near the centre of the historic burial ground, we approached a large pedestal monument, not noticing the name inscribed upon its marble scroll. What did capture our attention was a laminated piece of white paper, held down by a large river stone, but wildly flapping in a sudden gust of warm wind.

Intrigued, Allan picked up the white sheet and handed it to me. I took it in my hands, trying hard to make out the now blurry, and water-run words upon it. What was this, and why would someone place it on a grave, laminated to try and protect it from the elements., I went white, (whiter than usual) and Allan, having known me long enough by now, knew the look on my face meant something was going on.

"Allan, look at the name on the headstone," I almost whispered.

"Yeah, John Fleming, what about him?" He looked puzzled.

"Allan, listen to what this says."

I knew exactly who this person was, but could not believe that he was buried right here, in Wilberforce.

From memory, the faded piece of paper read: "Here lies John Henry Fleming, died 20th August 1894. One of 12 men who committed the brutal Myall Creek Massacre of Aboriginal people, at Myall Creek Station in 1838. Somehow, he escaped the hangman's noose to arrive here in the Hawkesbury, and be treated as a hero. People should know who this man was, and what he did. Lest we forget."

Allan knew about the Myall Creek Massacre, but didn't know the names of those involved. The discovery that we was standing at the grave of one of the perpetrators made his blood boil.

Shell-shocked at finding this man, in Wilberforce Cemetery of all places, we both shed tears of sadness, grief, and anger. Allan was overcome by an uncontrollable sense of rage, particularly at the knowledge that not only did John Fleming escape after his involvement in this deplorable act, but that he was welcomed to the area as a hero.

I turned to Allan, who was red-faced, and put my hand on his shoulder.

"Brother, it is good that we know the truth about what happened to this man, and where he ended up," I said.

"But in the end, he is here on the country and land that is proving itself to be somewhat like a blue print for the divergence of energies that are layering and building over time to capture and collect all of the energy needed to clear the pain of the past."

"The truth will be told my friend, and all souls, at some point, when the debt is paid, deserve the grace of forgiveness. Even this man. John Fleming. This is why we are here Allan; this is the task at hand."

"I know," he replied, still brewing.

"I just need to process it. I know."

We stood there for some time, amazed. I had walked through the cemetery many times and this piece of paper was never there. Strangely, the next time I returned it had disappeared. I will probably never know who put those words on that headstone. But whoever you were, you heard the call of spirit, helped us to find John, and in my heart of hearts I believe that paper played two roles: one, to tell the truth; two, to send a message to us, that John wanted to play his part in the unfolding dream, to be forgiven and to pay his debt in full.

It was all feeling more and more like a map created long before we came here, as there were now far too many synchronicities for it all to be a coincidence. It was in that moment that I had a vision of the land we were standing on, its energy layering and criss-crossing events, timelines and people. Like a map unfolding around me. This land that my ancestor was buried in was revealing pathways and the energies of all that was needed to collapse the old paradigm of pain. I didn't fully understand it, but it was starting to make itself known.

How vital it was, as a part of this process, to have John Fleming, one of the men who evaded the hangman's noose, like a symbol of the moment in time when the voices of our past became silenced. To me, the evidence was building that we were doing something that was beyond our comprehension on the spiritual plane. We left the cemetery and went across the road to the Wesleyan section to find yet another sign that we were on the right track.

As we walked the tree-lined path to the circle section of the block, Uncle Allan stopped and placed his hands in the red dirt beneath his feet. He called to us to take a look at what he had discovered, with a grin that only he and Uncle Greg could pull off. Laying his hand out to reveal his treasure, we saw an Australian $2 coin. On one side Gwoya Jungarai stood beneath the Southern Cross, long beard and powerful chest marked with tribal scars. Gwoya was the first Aboriginal to appear on a postage stamp, the survivor of one of the last recognised massacres of Aboriginals, and the face of a Central Australian tourism campaign.

Of course, we all know who is on the other side of the coin. The Queen of England, Elizabeth II. And so, there was the sign, confirmation we were on the right path: the two-sided coin.

Uncle Allan, the group and I stood humbly, as we turned to see a black and white feather, both the coin and feather laying in the middle of the circle of the land, almost waiting for us to find, and gather ourselves with the power of their symbolic confirmation that we could trust we were right on track and right on time.

We completed a simple prayer and smoking ceremony to clear the way for what would take place in the morning. It was important to ensure that all was ready for us to come together in love, peace and understanding. We left the land that day amazed and grateful for the unseen world, the connections and guidance that never failed to arrive right when we needed it.

The next morning, I awoke a little nervous and very excited, but mostly feeling the weight of what could unfold. I travelled with Uncle Allan and Uncle Greg and we arrived on country around 9am for the meeting. We introduced ourselves, and the Council representatives to the Friends of Wilberforce Cemetery, a gathering of about 10 descendants of settlers who were buried in the cemetery. They acted as a supporting body, raising money for necessary repairs and the like, but this was also a group of people who were very passionate about their history. I asked everyone to make a circle, stood in the middle and explained to everyone what we were hoping to achieve. I finished with my vision for a sandstone circle of peace, created and built by First Nations and First Settlers together, for the sake of healing the past for a better future.

There were a few questions, a little confusion, but by the end of my presentation, it was a powerful and resounding 'yes' from all. I had a moment where I felt like time stopped as I witnessed the ancestors of settlers standing arm in arm with Uncle Greg and Uncle Allan, joking and smiling together peacefully.

We all walked down the tree-lined alley way towards the circle in the middle, arm in arm, smiles for all and excitement for many. One woman in particular had tears welling in her eyes as she had thought that her dream of more than 13 years, to acknowledge the names of all those in the cemetery with the building of a monument would never be complete. Her husband beamed with joy that her task would be completed.

As we stood in a circle in the middle of the block, in the place where I saw the standing stones speak, I heard one man, who almost seemed to channel the voice of our ancient British past say: "Whoever agrees that this place becomes a sacred site of healing and remembrance for all, built together as one, say aye."

It was surreal as everyone lifted their hands and joyfully said as loud as they could, "Aye!"

And then we received our own confirmation. Just as we all cheered and raised our applause at the decision to move in the direction of creating a standing stone circle for peace, a huge truck passed us on the road carrying at least a dozen 6-foot-long, megalithic size sandstone blocks. As it drove past, we stood in shock, then looked at each other and burst out laughing. Some waved and called the truck to come back and deliver our stones. It was simply incredible.

There was still much work to do, many people to communicate with, and formal agreements to be made, but the seeds of love were sprouting, and the path began to unfold. For us, 9 February 2018 was an unforgettable day, when Indigenous Elders, the descendants of the First Settlers of the Hawkesbury, representatives of Hawkesbury Council, dear friends and soul family gathered together for the first time.

A space that would stand for our shared history, for the new dreaming of harmony and our walk together as One Mob. One shared history. One home, planet Earth. Standing as a monument in time, and a mark of the love of the descendants who came together as one. In a complete and moving consensus we chose to work towards the creation of a significant site of remembrance, healing and dreaming. The next step was to meet with other Indigenous Elders and more settler ancestors to share the dream and complete the circle.

I walked arm in arm with Uncle Greg to my car, a moment captured in a photo by the beautiful Roz Chia, journalist, magazine editor, and all-round inspirational woman. As I looked at the photo I thought if this is all we achieve, today was a miracle in time and space. And I am grateful, blessed and proud of all who were there that day. In that moment we really were, black, white, or any other shade of human, One Mob.

14

MR LINCOLN SPEAKS

"The trouble is you think you have time."

- JACK KORNFIELD

The 18th of April 2018 was the last day I would spend with my beloved father outside the confines of an Intensive Care, and ultimately Palliative Care ward in Orange Base Hospital. Dad had been in and out of hospital in Cowra and Orange for the last couple of months and had finally been allowed to go home as he was travelling so well. In the back of my mind, I knew that Dad's journey was coming to an end, though I still felt he would have at least six months to a year. He hadn't even begun the arduous process of chemotherapy or radiation, and yet in some ways it was the worst time of his life. We didn't realise until this very day that there was no time.

Dad had been discharged from Orange Base Hospital eight days earlier, feeling well and ready to go home to his humble abode. I picked him up on that beautiful Tuesday morning. He was happy, and excited to be getting out of hospital after a stressful few weeks filled with excruciating bone marrow scans, tests, and treatment for his Non-Hodgkin's

Lymphoma, which had horrifically swollen his legs, feet and abdomen. Finally, things were looking pretty good, he could get his shoes on at least, and walk relatively well. We drove home along the stunning country roads from Orange through Blayney and Cowra and eventually arrived in Grenfell, his home of more than 35 years.

Prior to that day he refused to go into the shops, would give me his card to purchase the meat and veggies we needed for a few days, sitting in the car while I went in. He was, as many of his vintage, a very proud man, extremely private, and knew he looked unwell. He didn't want people knowing his business or finding out that he could be terminally ill. Even he could not come to terms with his diagnosis, often telling me he had the 'non' type of Hodgkin's Lymphoma which meant it wasn't cancer. My father was no idiot. He just couldn't come to terms with it.

I guess after a lifetime of helping so many other people in different traumatic and life-threatening situations, he knew the back story, he knew how it went, and I don't blame him from trying to spare himself the fear of it all.

This day I was completely surprised that Dad wanted to come into the store with me, push the trolley and walk the aisle looking at all the colourful products and food on the shelves. In some ways it is one of my favourite memories of my father before he died. It would be the last time he would walk into that store, the last time he would chat with the locals about this and that, the last time he would bid the checkout lady goodbye and take up a conversation about the drought, the farmers, and of course that he had been in hospital, but was on the mend and feeling really good. Deep down though, he knew.

That night I cooked dinner the way Nan used to. A nice piece of scotch fillet steak. She used to cook it slow, which for most of us would be sacrilegious, but she did. Without fail she would place a steak on our plates that we would be able to cut with ease with one of her old butter knives. You know the ones with the bone handle and absolutely no serrated edges on it. It was always so tender and delicious. I did the meal he loved most – steak and veggies, mashed potato, peas and a little pumpkin. We sat down at the little round glass table that he had owned since God was a boy, and he spent the next 20 minutes telling me how he would never have been able to cook that, that he was tired, couldn't be bothered cooking and had been living on those king-size ready-made meals because he just couldn't get the energy to cook for himself. He was grateful, enjoyed it, but couldn't finish it.

I sat him on his favourite yellow lounge, pulled in a little table to put his swollen legs up and made him a cup of tea. With Dad comfortable at last, I left him to go to my room, catch up on a few emails and phone our family to let them know where we were at.

While on my last call, I heard something from the next room, but couldn't work out what it was, so I quickly wound up the conversation and went to check on Dad in case something had gone wrong.

What I saw next will stay with me for the rest of my days as one of the most heart-breaking experiences of my life. Here was my father, my rock, the strongest man I knew, the one I leant on and always knew would have my back and the right thing to say when things got tough. A man who had grown up in the harsh and back breaking days of the mid-1900s in Eugowra, on the NSW Central Western Plains. A farmer's son who had worked the fields on tractors, ploughing, and planting with his father Edward Shrimpton in the Australian heat and dust. He was tough, like most country people of those days were, and yet here was my father, frail, thin, and sobbing hysterically in that darn old yellow one-seater couch. I didn't know what I could say to him that might make matters any better. What could I say that wasn't a lie, something he knew wasn't true? The fact was he knew his time was short. No matter what was happening around him, he knew the battle was lost and he was terrified.

I knelt by his side for what seemed like an eternity, holding his head in my arms as he sobbed into my chest. In this moment everything changed. I knew the balance of power had fundamentally shifted, and from here on I, along with my sisters and family would have to become the stability and loving support that Dad needed. He could no longer be who he had been for us, and I would have to become the strong one, while my frail father became the one who needed nurturing.

I said nothing. I just held my tiny father who was once 6-feet tall, larger than life, with a smile that would light up a room and a laugh so infectious that everyone would join in, even if what he was laughing at wasn't funny. Eventually the waves of pain, fear and sorrow passed. He calmed down in my arms and settled. I said the only thing that I felt could make a difference.

"Would you like a cup of tea?"

"Yes, please that would be nice," he replied, drying his red eyes and blowing his nose.

I walked out into the kitchen and grabbed the lighter – Dad had one of those old-fashioned gas stoves that needed a lighter to start it. He also had an old whistle kettle, which I filled with water, and placed on the stove. There is something so comforting in that action. For generations we have offered a cup of tea as a way of comforting a weary traveller, someone who has had a long day, or someone who is in pain. This action is something that lies deep in our DNA.

Dad got himself up and walked into the kitchen and lent against the peach-coloured bench beside the sink. I'm sure he was embarrassed, but also relieved. When I look back on it, I am honoured that he felt safe enough, inside his stoic way of being, to allow me to see him at his most vulnerable. And it was also in this moment that we turned a massive corner in the experience of true, unconditional love.

"I feel so much better now, I really needed to let that out."

"Yes, Dad, it's really important to let our emotions go, it's healing and helps us to cope."

"Yes. And I'm not one to cry. My father didn't cry, his father didn't cry. And I don't like to cry. But I do feel better."

And that was that, we didn't speak of it again. He went for a shower and I helped him get ready for bed. By this time his legs were swollen and sore. They could barely bend and he would scream and cry in agony. There is a huge difference between pain and agony, and agony is excruciating for both those suffering, and those witnessing it. Finally, we had him in bed, and I made my way to my little bedroom at the back of the house.

The bed in this room was tiny. It had belonged to my grandmother, Elva Mary Shrimpton, and Dad kept it in his spare room made up with her floral bed covers. I crawled in, exhausted and, for the first time, truly scared. Questioning whether I was up to this journey. I vividly remember laying there as I turned out the light thinking to myself, "I cannot do this, don't make me do this, don't make me watch this, I can't watch him die. I just can't." Matters were made worse during that night, and all the nights I stayed at my father's house caring for him in the weeks and months leading to his passing, listening to the sounds of him weep, sob and cry out in pain. Sometimes I would go into him to make sure he was okay, and other times, I am ashamed to say I would put the earphones into my ears and listen to something, anything, other than the sound of my father's cries all night long.

The next morning, once I knew for sure Dad could cope, and that there were services in place to support him, I travelled back to Sydney to work for a few days. At that stage I was still working and I didn't want to let my business partner down. That day I was given at least four signs that Dad's time was short, the ancestors were gathering closely to us both, and preparing him for his journey home. The first sign was when I woke up and went into Dad's room to help him out of his bed. We pulled back his charcoal coloured covers to reveal the fluid and blood on the sheets that was weeping from his swollen legs. It took him what seemed like an eternity to sit up, bend his legs, and get up to go to the bathroom. The pain was beyond what I truly believe anyone should be required to experience, but it was as it was. He came back into the bedroom as I stripped the sheets and prepared to wash them, and he asked a question.

"Did you come into my room early this morning?"

"No Dad, I didn't."

"You must have" he said, "because there was someone sitting on the edge of my bed around dawn this morning. I saw them! You must have."

"No, Dad, I promise I didn't come in at all last night," I said as he looked at me completely confused and bewildered.

"The mind boggles," he said, and I agreed, thinking to myself that there was a chance that he may have had a visit. Either from the elderly lady that lived there before him, or one of the women in our family line. Most probably his mother.

"Did you get a chance to see who it might be?" I asked gently, knowing he was far from a spiritual person, even though his mother was a devotee of the Legion of Mary. She was a loving, spiritual soul who prayed much and believed deeply in her faith. He became a little annoyed with me, as my dad often did when questioned.

"I don't know," he said.

"If you could imagine who it was, could you?"

"Oh, I don't know," he said, "maybe she was older. An older lady I guess."

He went to the kitchen – obviously that conversation was over. But what I knew for sure was that Dad's time was near. For someone who was distinctly unspiritual, not interested in these matters, and relatively sceptical , to have a vision of a woman sitting on the edge of his bed told me his loved ones on the other side of the veil were growing near and preparing him subconsciously for his journey. Helping him to see he would not be alone, and as much as the transition would be frightening, they were trying to show him they were waiting, and he would be okay.

The second sign was in the form of Dad having a huge argument with his clock. Because he had not been home for some time, and daylight savings had changed our time by an hour he needed to go around the house and change the clocks one by one. And one by one he struggled. I realised then that he was becoming confused, struggling to write and recall information and dates, and doing strange things that he had never done before. Struggling with clocks was one of them. He was angry, yelling in his room at the clock on his bedside, "Why can't I change the time?" I didn't think much of it the first time. Then he completed his task and moved to the kitchen to change the clock that now hangs above me in my office and clinic room. Again, the fight began, and I tried to ignore his huge temper tantrum as he again screamed, "Why can't I change the time?" The third time I was at my car placing the last few items I needed to get back to Sydney for a few days before returning to meet him in Cowra.

There he was sitting in his car once again out of control screaming "Why can't I change the time?" Almost in tears. And then I finally heard it. It is his time. I stood behind his car as he finally got the job done and he walked out to say our goodbyes. I could see he was afraid to be in the house on his own, and I felt absolutely horrible leaving to try and keep a small part of my own life running. But the bills needed to be paid, and the clinic costs needed to be covered. I hated the drive home along the Cowra Road that day, leaving him alone, though I comforted myself with the knowledge that I would get a few things done and be back in a few days to be with Dad for his next appointment, and as he began his long-term treatments of chemo and radiation. As much as I still thought we had a long journey of treatments ahead, deep down I knew the messages from spirit were trying to give me a heads up. It was time, and time was short.

So a few days later, on 18 April 2018, my husband Steve and I jumped in the car to drive to Cowra and meet Dad for his appointment with his haematologist who had news of his bone scan, and pathway ahead. We arrived in Cowra at about 11am, 20 minutes ahead of time. We walked through the halls of the hospital and found him waiting outside the doctor's office. He looked well, happy, and in good spirits. The Doctor opened her door and we walked in to be confronted with the information that the cancer had spread to Dad's bones. Dad sat quietly and didn't say much as the doctor explained that he would now need to eat well and prepare for the next stage, a very light round of chemotherapy. Honestly, seeing Dad struggle as it was, I really didn't think he would survive the chemo or cope with more suffering. The plan was to wait a couple of weeks, try and get some more weight on, and go back into hospital at the start of May for surgery to fix some oesophageal varices that they were concerned could burst and cause Dad to bleed out under chemo. In the meantime, he was to have a flu shot.

The doctor was happy with how Dad looked, and seemed positive about the whole scenario, but one wonders whether they knew there was no hope for him, and were just going through the motions to have him feel better about it. Dad was not ready to go, but who is I guess.

We drove to the famous Rose Garden Cafe in Cowra to spend some time together, have a cup of tea, and discuss the outcome and plans.

Dad sat quietly and asked me, "What did she say again?"

"Dad," I replied with as much compassion as possible, "She said they found it in your bones."

"Yes, that's right," he said.

What else was there to say? I had nothing. I felt completely lost for words.

I eventually said, "Well, let's just keep taking one day at a time, we will have you relax, eat well, get well and prepare for the next part of your journey. In the meantime, shall we go and walk in the rose garden?"

And so we walked out into the garden on a beautiful day to spend what would be our final moments together in the sun. In spite of all that was going on, we stopped to smell the roses, found beauty in the moment, and stood in awe of the miracle of nature and our joint love of roses. In particular Mr Lincoln. The Cowra Rose Garden is a popular attraction that contains approximately 880 bushes of 130 varieties, including a bed of the beautiful Cowra Rose.

We were particularly lucky that day as the flowers are at their best between late October and May. It was April, and there were thousands of beautiful blooms of every shape, colour and size. As we became lost in the rose bushes it was almost possible to forget why we were there, what we had just found out, and what we were about to face in the coming days. I could hear Dad walking behind me talking about how deeply he loved the rose, Mr Lincoln, and not only that, that it was his mother's favourite rose. My favourite also.

Mr Lincoln roses produce very large dark red blooms that average

5 inches in diameter and are very full with 35 to 40 petals per bloom. It has a strong, damask scent and is often grown for cut flowers in arrangements. Gardeners often grow this rose near a patio or a window so they can enjoy its strong scent even when they aren't standing directly beside it. It has a dark blood red colour with velvety petals and it is easy to understand why it was so loved through our family's generations.

I could hear Dad in the background, still talking about this and that, and about Mr Lincoln, as we wandered through the garden seeing every rose but the Mr Lincoln. Now remember this is a huge garden of 880 rose bushes. We were at one end of the garden, when I felt called to walk to the other end. As I walked, still hearing Dad bang on and on about Mr Lincoln I could see a red rose reaching high into the sky, so high I found it hard to reach up and gently pull it down just to smell it and take a photo. I had no intention whatsoever to pick it, nor had I checked to see what type of rose it was. As I pulled it down to see it the whole branch broke away from the plant. A stem at least a meter long, just lifted away from the bush as if handed to me as a gift. Every other time I have tried to pick a rose without scissors it has been a fight to the death, usually ending up with a few thorns in my fingers. This was really strange.

Dad was horrified that I had broken the plant (completely unintentionally). I felt horrible and quickly resorted to trying to pluck the rose from its stem and put the bush down. As Dad approached me, I looked down to the ground to see what the name of the rose was, and of course, it was our Mr Lincoln. Dad arrived at my side still giving me a mouthful for harming the plant.

I turned to him and said, "Guess what rose this is?"

He looked down, his eyes widened, and he blurted out what he usually said when something really amazed him.

"Strike! Holy Suffering Toledo! The mind boggles!"

I handed him the rose and said, "Here, a gift from Nan."

He took the rose and we wandered through the rest of the garden, amazed that of the 880 roses, this one called us, and gifted itself to us, and turned out to be my father's, his mother's, and her mother's favourite. The one he so desperately wished to see that day, and the one that led us straight to it. I felt like those on the other side of the veil had reached through to hand us that rose, and for me it was one more strong sign that time was short and our ancestors were coming in close to support, guide and prepare us for what was about to happen.

For a brief moment we all went from feeling that sober sadness of uncomfortable news to wonder and awe of the miracles of life in the simplest of moments, and how profoundly they can touch us. I cherish the memory of that day. Our final time together, outside enjoying the beauty of nature, fresh air and one another's company.

We went back to our cars: Steve and I needed to journey back to Sydney, and Dad needed to head home. I would be travelling out to see him again in a few days. I cannot imagine how difficult it must have been for him in his final days at home alone, and the one regret I have is that I didn't listen hard enough to the messages, to get out there and not leave him alone for one moment. But we live and learn and try to choose more wisely the next time we are faced with impossible decisions when trying to make it all work, trying not to let others down in the process, and allowing ourselves to focus wholly on time with our loved ones. No matter what the circumstances, if we all lived in such a way, always, maybe we could avoid the pitfalls of regret and pain.

At our cars, my father cried as he held me. He knew, and he was suddenly so grateful.

He looked at me with his big blue eyes and said, "Thank you Ange."

He looked at my husband Steve and said, "This one," while motioning toward me.

He couldn't quite say it. His heart was in a complex moment of what seemed like deep gratitude, sadness, and grief all at once. Having that sliding door moment where you are so proud of someone, so grateful for what they have done for you. We said our goodbyes and went our separate ways.

As we journeyed along the country road towards Bathurst I spoke about the signs, and that I felt his time was much nearer than we could imagine. All of a sudden there was an eagle, a huge bird dead on the road. I called out to Steve to stop! We couldn't have been even 10 kilometres out of Cowra when this bird presented itself. I pulled it to the side of the road and saw that it was perfect in every way. No blood, it just looked like it was sleeping, and had only died a few moments ago. Maybe it was hit, who knows, but here it was, an Eagle lying on the side of the road. For some this would not be t anything to write home about, but in that moment I knew. I saw the sign with more clarity than I had ever before. Dad was about to get his unrestricted licence to fly. Fly home.

I see signs and messages in animals, trees, plants and birds. The pieces of the puzzle were clear to me. Many years before, on 23 January 1992 my father had completed his training to become a pilot and did an alone-and-unassisted take-off and return to Parkes Airport, completing his very first solo flight and becoming qualified. Flying was the love of my father's life.

When I was 16 years old, I gave him a gift to celebrate his amazing achievement. The gift I gave him was a little stuffed eagle, to hang in his plane when he flew. He cherished it and ended up naming it 'Little Eagle.' Dad also received a certificate that he talked about almost every time we spoke of flying or doing something new that we were afraid of. The certificate had a picture of an eagle kicking a baby eagle out of the nest to soar. He would laugh uncontrollably over this certificate, seeing himself as the baby eagle ready to fly but afraid to leap. A good kick up the 'you know what' was required.

As time collapsed in front of me, I realised that the eagle we stood over on the side of the road was indeed an Australian Little Eagle. I knew Dad was about to take his last solo flight home, and he was going soon. I turned to Steve and said, "he is going, and he is going solo really soon." Steve looked at me as if he wasn't really sure. I sat in silence the whole way home knowing that I now needed to prepare myself to lose my best friend, my support, my guide, and my father far sooner than he or I wanted. It was his time. Ready or not.

That night I closed my eyes to find myself inside a really clear vision of my grandmother, Elva Mary Shrimpton. We chatted about all sorts of things, but one thing I did ask her was what was happening with Aunty Pam? Why is she waiting to pass? She has said all of her goodbyes, even to her brother, my Dad. Why? You see Dad's sister had been in Palliative Care for quite some time, and for all intents and purposes she had been on death's door for months. The doctors couldn't believe how long she was continuing to live, and in some ways, were puzzled at her strength to keep going.

Nanna Shrimpton simply turned to me with a smile and said, "Angela, she is waiting for Colin."

"No, that cannot be because she is ready to go, and Dad could have months or a year ahead."

"No," she said. "She is waiting for Colin and they will cross over together."

I woke up in tears after experiencing what felt like a real conversation with my Nanna, and in all honesty, I truly believe that I did speak with her. True to her word, Aunty Pam passed away on 26 April 2018, and her little brother, my Dad, followed just days later on 1 May 2018 at exactly 4.04pm. It was one of the most difficult conversations I have ever had, to tell him on his death bed of the loss of his sister, and yet, I felt a certain peace to know that she was there in the wings waiting for him, to hold his hand so they could go home together. I knew she held on so that he would not have to make the journey across the bridge on his own, because he was so afraid.

In the end, we can even defy death, as Aunty Pam did, so that love wins.

15

BACK ON COUNTRY

"My dreaming brought me home."

— UNCLE BOB RANDALL

After what seemed like a whirlwind week, which felt like falling into the mouth of hell, we left the hospital where Dad had died and made our way back to Grenfell, to my father's home. It is a strange experience going back to the home of someone who has passed away. Their clothes lying where they last dropped them, their towel hanging from the last time they showered, their favourite items by their bedside, the paper on the dining table, their coffee cup waiting on the sink. Dad's calendar on the wall told me all the appointments he had scheduled for that day. I could see him, smell him and feel him all around me but somehow, in less than a second he had disappeared, leaving his entire life, belongings, and countless memories.

That darn bright yellow one-seater couch that he had sat in for as long as I could remember was empty, the shape of his body moulded into its worn fabric and contours. There were blood stains on the arms from where Dad's paper-thin skin had bled simply from the pressure of him leaning on them to steady him as he stood. In his final days in his home, he slept on the three-seater couch in the lounge room, he just couldn't put himself to bed at night. Was he afraid to die in bed? Did he somehow believe if he stayed on the couch, he would have more chance of living?

Maybe it was just more comfortable, maybe being in front of the TV helped when sleep eluded him. Whatever it was, I couldn't wait to be rid of that yellow couch, and in the coming days I would push it onto a pile of rubbish at the tip and watch it being destroyed from the rear-view mirror of his little red Nissan Ute. In that same rear-view mirror, I saw a man walk over to find one of Dad's very old, and unusable motor bike helmets, one of many that he had owned during a lifetime as a motorcycle lover. That grey and black helmet with a red strip was way too big for me as a child, and when he collected me every second weekend to visit with my grandmother Elva, he would place that helmet on my little head. As we rode, the wind would spin it sideways and block my view, but I didn't care. I was with my Dad, and regardless of how cold or windy it was on the back of that bike, I would put my little hands inside the pockets of his leather jacket and many times fell asleep.

Seeing a stranger, in a tip, pick up that poignant part of my childhood was like watching timelines collapsing. My whole existence rotated in space and I felt the immeasurable reality of my loss. My life was becoming a mirage of memories that with every moment longer that Dad was gone, began to wobble and fade.

Sleeping in Dad's bed the first night after he died was traumatic. I woke several times and would swear I could hear him calling me and sobbing in the night. I had to leave the lights on, I couldn't close my eyes without going back to the last moments we had spent in that house. I could hear, see and feel it like it was still happening. I must have finally gone to sleep in the early hours of the morning, as I believe I woke up around dawn, slipped out of bed and headed to the front door. When I woke up from what I am about to share with you I couldn't work out whether I dreamt it, or if I actually did get out of bed and walk to the front yard of my Dad's house.

So I guess you could say I had a vision, as it didn't feel in any way, shape or form that I was dreaming. This happens to me from time to time, and I find my visions to be distinct in their nature, and different in every way that they are perceived. This is where we can begin to recognise the moments in time when the ancestors, source, great spirit or God, whatever it is that you call the creator, the energy that we all are, always have been and always will be, reaching through to communicate.

I had a vision that I woke up in the early hours of the morning, the sun had just started to come up, I could smell the dew in the air and hear the plentiful birds outside my father's bedroom window that just do not exist in Sydney. I sat up, twisted my legs out of bed and walked to the front door. I opened it and stood there surveying the front yard, which was dry, with barely a blade of grass across its entirety, the drought in the area playing havoc. Dad and I had numerous conversations about how dry the land was, and if I went out to water the plants, he would call out "Don't bother, it doesn't make a difference." But I would still water the little shrubs and plants to try and give them something to keep them going. It was dusty, dry and desolate.

As I looked across the yard, I noticed in the top left-hand corner a small group of Aboriginal men and women. They were sitting in a small circle and enjoying the rising of Grandfather Sun, as Uncle Greg Simms would call it. As soon as I saw them, they turned and waved me to come over. I walked across the yard, filled with catheads, bindies, and burrs without a second thought, and arrived beside them as they turned to greet me.

"Hey, welcome home, where ya been?" One older man asked me.

They motioned me to join the circle and sit down with them in the dry red dirt.

"Hey, thank you." I said. "Dad passed away two days ago, I have been caring for him for some time now and he went home to the ancestors and his family on Tuesday."

"Angela, this is your country you know; you know what to do on that land now don't you."

And with a start I woke up, the voice of the old Aboriginal man ringing in my head. It was like a speaker phone was vibrating through my ears and booming into my chest. My heart was pounding, and it took me a moment to work out where I was. Was I dreaming? Did I get up? Did I walk outside and have a conversation out in the front yard? To this day I don't know. What I did know was that the pathway continued, that all was perfect, that I was being guided, supported and led by the ancestors, both my own familiar ones, and countless others who stood for the outcome we dreamt of - truth, forgiveness, love, and unity.

As I acknowledged all the spirits who were guiding me, I thought there might be a period where Dad would need to adjust to his new reality, that I might not see any signs from him for a while. To my surprise he would immediately become more present, and more able in some ways to guide and help me achieve our great aim than when he was alive, and he proved without a doubt from the moment he took his last breath that he was there, and would communicate more succinctly and powerfully than I ever imagined he could.

That is where the Maltese Cross comes in, his sign, and way of telling me he is near. And more than this, it was time to write to the Queen again.

16

THE MALTESE CROSS

"Every night I lie in bed, the brightest colours fill my head, a million dreams keeping me awake. I think of what the world could be, a vision of the one I see. A million dreams are all it's going to take. A million dreams for the world we are going to make."

- THE GREATEST SHOWMAN

A few months after Dad died, a company I worked with asked me if I would like to present a Community Service Award in my father's name, The Colin Shrimpton Community Service Award for 2018. Of course, I was overjoyed to do so, and happily prepared a speech to present this award to a man who, I learned two days before the event, was also a long time paramedic, now working with helicopter rescue teams. I handed him my father's Ambulance Service Crests and award, the recipient speechless and moved to tears. From that moment we shared a bond through his understanding of the life my father led as a paramedic. The loss, the pain, the stress of seeing people suffer is often difficult to bear.

I had a gut feeling that this man would become a part of my greater journey, though I had no idea how or why. We even had a really freaky experience when he shared a photo of himself and his co-workers in front of an ambulance helicopter. I sent back a very old black and white photo of my father and his co-worker handing over a patient from their ambulance to a helicopter.

"Hey, check out this old picture of my Dad!"

"Oh my God, Angela, you won't believe this! That helicopter is the exact same one in the picture I just sent you, and I am positive that the man in the black jumpsuit taking the patient from your father is me!"

Buckingham Palace
LONDON
SW 1A 1AA

March 30th, 2019

Your Majesty,

Thank you sincerely for taking the time to read this correspondence once again. I wrote to you in earnest last year, in regards to an important object I wished to bring to your attention. I hope you may reconsider at the conclusion of this letter. The Maltese Cross that bears so much significance to Royal orders, seals and symbols, stands out most poignantly to me, as I look at a photograph of my father, the late Colin Anthony Shrimpton, who was a Paramedic with New South Wales Ambulance for more than 34 years. He received a medal of honour for his long and dedicated service to his community here in Australia.

Unfortunately, my father passed away on 1 May 2018. After so many years of service it was our time to serve him as he left this world. I am so broken hearted that he will not physically be here on this journey to complete this great task with me, but I send his badge bearing the Maltese Cross as a bridge between us. That cross being born upon orders and awards this world knows to be of great honour. Of humanitarianism, truth, love, dedication, faith and courage. It is not mine to bear, but his to gift. There was nothing my father loved more than serving his community and saving lives. Each and every time I see that Maltese Cross, I think of my father, and its place on the New South Wales Ambulance emblem. I now see its significance to your order, to the Crown and honour.

In all honesty as I received your letter, I felt a great sadness, and defeat. After a long year of caring for my dying father, and many years of being guided to this moment in time, failure is not an option. I couldn't begin to explain how many years this has been coming together. It is a huge task that I feel dwarfed by. So many synchronicities, so many miraculous connections and moments that have kept me going.

This must become something more than a miracle in my mind, but I must admit I felt it was time to give up and stop dreaming. One person simply cannot make this sort of difference, and the last spark of hope was lost with the thought that our leaders and those we look up to and admire don't actually care. I felt this way for but a moment, until an Ambulance passed me by as I stood with your letter in my hands, that Maltese Cross ever guiding me.[1]

We are all familiar with the Maltese cross, you more than most, but I failed to know its full history or even why our Paramedics came to wear this striking symbol on their uniforms. Travelling back in time to the 11th Century, The Sistine Chapel is yet to be built (Michelangelo not yet famous for his masterpiece), the Arnhem Land Plateau already features rock art depicting the didgeridoo, and William the Conqueror has the 1066 Battle of Hastings still fresh in his mind. The year is 1099 and hordes of crusaders left Western Europe to travel towards Constantinople (modern-day Istanbul) and then, onto Jerusalem. The crusaders arrive in Jerusalem amidst this tumultuous backdrop, while a group of monks are giving aid to ill pilgrims just as they have done for centuries. As the crusaders arrived, these monks would go to support those injured and requiring treatment. The 'Knights of the Order of St. John of

Jerusalem' (as the monks were officially called) braved the battlefields and tended to the sick and injured, realising two vital points: Firstly, they would need to protect themselves, and secondly, they needed to wear a symbol that sent the message on the dangerous fields that they were friend, not foe. In fact, their lives depended on it. So, it was to be that the Cross of Calvary would accompany them to the front lines of battle in the name of first aid. The knights received status that was the envy of kings, princes and princesses.[2]

Within this historical context, we can now place the Ambulance Service of NSW in the picture, where my father served for many years. One of my first memories is that Cross on his shoulder. If we fast forward several hundred years, to 1895, we arrive in a police station near Central in the heart of Sydney. This was Australia's very first Ambulance Station. Back then, two permanent officers rode in horse drawn carts and were on-call to respond to medical emergencies of all kinds. 'Ambulance Bearers' (as they were then called) wore a red cross on their badge to signify their humanitarian role and intention to be of aid to others. The Maltese Cross is indeed an admirable symbol in support of an honourable vocation; a vocation which (officially, at least) began close to 1000 years ago or more.[3]

What does all of this have to do with my request? The Maltese Cross is bestowed to those whom the Queen holds in high regard, to those exhibiting bravery, loyalty, contribution of all kinds to humanity and more, its foundation upon the Maltese cross, a symbol of divinity of the highest order to some.

I call in divinity of the highest order in this instance for all those who have ears to hear. My father lived his life within its principles of service, as now do I, and I hand it to you to trigger and uphold the most divine response available to you. I implore you to let this cross shine ever brighter in its quest to be truly majestic. The only other thing my father loved more than serving others was discovering his ancestry and our family history. He was so very proud of our so-called less than desirable 'convict roots,' and so very humbled at all we as Australians have created in just over 230 years.

We as a country are at a critical point in our history, our people are seeking truth, our ancestors are seeking forgiveness, and our future generations are seeking peace. It is our responsibility, as the current generation to do all we can to leave the world less divided and less perilous than when we entered, even if it was not our actions that caused this division. One small, yet monumental part of this complex puzzle of forging peace between our First Nations people, settlers, all Australians and Crown is the letter of apology. I truly understand that in one moment in time, what one believes is best, just and most helpful, may seem different through the eyes of the lens of the future, and that Her Majesty cannot be blamed, in the same way that I cannot be blamed for the actions of my ancestors. But we can seek to learn, to have compassion, grow, improve and evolve, and in doing so build upon a past with a healed present with the better judgement of our times.

In light of all this, I will ask again, and continue to ask until I receive the answer I seek. I realise that I asked much in my first letter. And so, I will reduce my request to but one great object at this time: The apology to Australia's First Nations people, stating the profound regret for the loss of lives due to the hostilities arising from the invasion and devastation of property and culture, which resulted on their lands. I will again stress that while the document would be in the name of the Crown, it is not a personal apology from the Queen. I understand the Queen acts through her Government and does not do things personally. I wish to advise that on its completion I will travel from Australia to London, to journey to the gates of Buckingham Palace to be handed the official and original letter to collect and return to Australia. I dream of that day and stand firm in my belief that it is not only possible but inevitable. As an act of love and reconciliation, as part of the national process of the regrettable injustices of the past, for the gift of a more prosperous present. This moral and ethical act of good conscience and demonstration of respect of all humanity, has the overall goal of restoring dignity and sound harmony to our people.

Thomas Jefferson once said, "I tremble for my country when I consider God is just, and his justice shall not sleep forever." I tremble with him as I see the past injustices begin to awaken in the hearts and minds of the people. Many generations have done much to restore and atone for our past, but that does not mean that it would be wise to turn our backs on what it is for our generation to do for the sake of love, peace and a better world.

Pope John Paul used a powerful term, the Purification of Memory.[4] He believed that if you do not apologise for wrongful action, you will remain oblivious to the fact that you are continuing to do it. The way things are now in Australia reveals the effect of the cause, and the cause isn't ultimately about what we did or didn't do all those years ago. The cause was the consciousness of the people of the time, and it was this consciousness that created and exacerbated the effect.

As Abraham Lincoln said:

"We have been preserved all these years in peace and prosperity, grown in numbers wealth and power, but we have forgotten God, we have forgotten the gracious hand that has preserved us in peace and multiplied and strengthened and enriched us and we have vainly imagined in the deceitfulness of our hearts that all these blessings were produced by some superior wisdom of our own. Intoxicated with our own unbroken success we have become too self-sufficient to feel the necessity of redeeming and preserving grace, too proud to say to the God who made us, too proud to pray. It behoves us then to humble ourselves before the offended power our national sins. The notion of collectively confessing our sins, and to pray for clemency and forgiveness. It is the duty of nations, as well of men to confess their sins and transgressions in humble sorrow, yet with genuine repentance that will lead to mercy and pardon."

Robert Kennedy said there was a belief that there was nothing one person could do against the enormous array of the world's ills, misery, ignorance, injustice and violence. Yet, he pointed out that many of the world's great movements of thought and action often flowed from the work of a single human being, such as a young monk who began the protestant reformation, a young woman who reclaimed the territory of

France, and the 32-year-old Thomas Jefferson who proclaimed that all men were created equal.

Kennedy reminds us, "that we each can work to change a small portion of events in the hope that all of these acts be written in the history of that generation. Each time a man stands up for an ideal, acts to improve the lives of others, and strikes out against injustice, he sends forth a tiny ripple of hope; and crossing each other from a million different centres of energy and daring, those ripples build a current that can sweep down the mightiest walls of oppression and resistance."

May this letter, this one person, a no-one really, be someone, do something that in generations to come will mean something. Kennedy reminds us that it takes great courage and self-confidence to overcome this fear, but that only those who dare to fail greatly, can ever achieve greatly. Few men are willing to face the disapproval of their fellows, the wrath of their society, moral courage being a rarer commodity than bravery in battle or great intelligence. It is, Kennedy says, "the one essential, vital quality for those who seek to change the world, which yields most painfully to change."

I send this Maltese Cross, worn with pride by my father, to you as a sign that I am friend not foe, and to signify my humanitarian intentions and request, to note my real concern for the welfare of others, of my people, my nation, and humbly say that our lives, our future surely does depend on the answer to this small, yet remarkable request. I hope that this symbol, which graces so many of your most honourable orders. may inspire thee to take the greatest step, the most divine expression towards the most honourable, beautiful and profound outcome. For as Kennedy reminds us:

"The energy, faith, and devotion which we bring to this endeavour will light our country and all who serve it, and the glow from that fire can truly light the world. A good conscience our only sure reward, with history the final judge of our deeds, let us move forward to lead the land we love, asking for his blessing and his love, but knowing that here on earth God's work must truly be our own."
(Kennedy, Robert, 1966. Speech for Humanity.)

May this work be truly my own, may God save and bless you.
Yours Sincerely,

Angela Mary Sciberras

The Queen Replies
9th April 2019

Dear Mrs Sciberras,

The Queen has asked me to thank you for your letter of 30th March, and to say that Her Majesty has taken careful note of the views you express. Perhaps I might explain, however, that this is not a matter in which The Queen would intervene. As a constitutional Sovereign, Her Majesty acts through her personal representative, the Governor General, on the advice of her Australian Ministers and, therefore, it is to them that your appeal should be directed. I am, therefore, returning for your safe keeping the New South Wales Ambulance Badge which you enclosed with your letter. Her Majesty was sorry to learn of the death of your beloved father Mr Colin Shrimpton, last year and The Queen has asked me to convey her sympathy to you for such a deep loss.

Yours sincerely,
Jennie Vine
Chief Correspondence Co-ordinator

17

THE PROPHESY IN THE PAINTING

"Your personal legend is the reason you are here. You are here to honour something called the miracle of life. You know deep inside there is something that you are meant to do here."

- PAULO COELHO

After my father died there was a void. An empty space that just could not be filled, and yet it is a pivotal and extremely important part of this journey. It was the moment in time that someone else, completely unknown to me, confirmed in a very powerful and visual way what I had believed all along. I had a purpose, and I was being guided to complete it every step of the way.

The most important part of this process is to say that I was not aware of the deeper details of the historical, or mythical nature of what ended up being portrayed of me in the painting. I need to make this extremely clear that as much as I had some knowledge in regards to the symbols and time frame I was depicted, I had no idea of the depth of the myth, the true meaning of the symbols, and how inexplicably powerful their message about my role would be.

My friend Lindy had met a woman named Francine t and that meeting would be the next joined dot of my quest: the teacher always appears when the student or soul is ready. One Friday evening in November 2018, after a beautiful meditation and cherished time with my dear friends Lindy and Mervyn, I prepared for bed in the very back room of their house, listening to the ocean crashing against the rocks only meters from my window, and smelling the salt air wafting through the newly hung white blinds.

Having spoken to Lindy about her new acquaintance, I sat down to write an email to Francine to request a Soul Light Portrait. Maybe it would help me see the light within myself again. Maybe it would reconnect me to my path after feeling like my world had come crashing down around me, leaving nothing but dust and rubble. I had lost faith in myself, in the world, in others and most of all, in my purpose. At the very least, it would be fun to see myself through the eyes of another. I clicked send and turned off the light, the sounds of the waves washing over me as I drifted off to sleep.

Francine was moving, busy and about to leave for overseas and we were not even sure if she would be continuing to do the paintings at all. But I received an email back the next morning, and having remembered Lindy, Francine was only too happy to book me in. It would, however, be a while before she could get around to completing the portrait. She said she would contact me when she had moved and settled, and as I was in no rush, I let it go and completely forgot about it.

On 1 May 2019, the first anniversary of my father's passing I recalled making the booking with Francine and wondered how she was travelling. I dropped her a line. By the next day we had a time booked for to complete the initial part of the process of creating this vision and artwork. In the end it was perfect that so much time had passed. The session was intense with huge amounts of different energies crowding around before and during. There was an enormous amount of people in spirit, which Francine found a little overwhelming.

Generally, she would see a few spirits, masters or energies step forward clearly, but in my case, there were many crowding in at once, presenting as a big group, showing a lot of support. Francine immediately felt the energy of Brigid, a Druid warrior, come through to calm things and bring in softness and patience, like she was speaking to me and every other soul there with me, settling the chaos. Francine told me the process I was about to complete was being overseen by my main Indigenous female guides, as well as Brigid and the Divine Mothers, Mother Mary and Hathor. She told me that Archangel Michael was with me, protecting me. We completed a meditation and clearance, and Francine took her leave to have time to create and channel the painting.

The painting was said to represent me as a multidimensional being of light. In this form I hold eternal wisdom and grace. Grace is our natural state of being, our home within. In all honesty I felt far from grace, and less graceful than ever in my life. "This is how you work and move within the world of form. Not many can flow so gracefully, and yet be so powerful to affect change. And yet this is what your soul is here to do," Francine explained.

It would take weeks for me to truly understand the significance of the symbols in the painting. I am depicted standing strong and ready with my own sword of "Excalibur" or truth. My truth extends to what is right for all as I develop a great mature understanding and experience of oneness. The many personal trials I had faced had increased my ability to love, and opened my heart wider, although I was told it might not feel that way just yet. And she was right, at that time, and still a little today my heart feels closed, afraid to open and let others in once again. The painting is mostly green, brown and gold, the colours of earthly love, the beloved Mother Earth and spiritual wisdom and attainment. Many presented at the session but not all could come through to speak. The main women who Francine saw watching over me and my energy field were Hathor, and Brigid. Brigid guides my adventures in creating change in the world, standing up for what is truly right. She assists me with courage and mental agility to see the task through to the end.

I now know that I have at least 36% Irish and Scottish ancestry in my blood, and 56% English, and Wales, so I am not surprised that Brigid plays such an important role. But I had no idea who she was when I first read this information. I also have about 8% Nordic ancestry, which it seems is also interesting. There is endless information about Brigid, but to give you a basic idea, she is a Celtic Goddess, who was worshipped by both the Goidelic and Brythonic Celts in the British Isles and beyond. The word 'brigand' comes from this tribe of fierce warriors. The symbol of Britain — the Goddess Brigantia or Britannia, (still found on their fifty-cent coin) is Brigid in her aspect as the Goddess of Sovereignty or Guardian of the Land.[1]

I was altogether blown away at the constant, and powerful connections, guidance and symbols surrounding this journey. The white dove of purity flies on my left, of course representing the purity of my intentions ("no need to doubt these," said Francine), along with the purity of my heart as an instrument of peace and healing.

Royalty was the word that came through often during the painting process, and Francine was to paint me regally, with the clothes of a Master of Light who has passed many grades. Francine explained that Stag is the symbol and "cue" of my father and grandfather's, and that I needed to be aware that they will use numbers to connect with me when the time is divinely right. The number four is the alignment number, or anything between 404 and 444. Messages from beyond will take the form of numbers such as: 44, 404, 444 — asking me to stand proud and stand tall, to remind me I am protected, they are with me, and they are near. The numbers 411 and 414 are the message to keep going, to show I'm on the right track and aligned.

The numbers 424 will be about decisions or crossroads, a reminder to choose wisely when these numbers show themselves. The numbers 434 draw on my divine feminine energy and maternal bloodline. Lastly, 444 draws on the masculine energies in your paternal bloodline. I am not surprised about these numbers, as my father passed away on the timeline portal of 4.04pm on 1 May 2018.

Francine was guided to form a ring of carnelian around me on the painting, the crystal of victory and success, as well as nurturing of the divine feminine sacral chakra. These have been placed there to allow me to authentically soften into the strength of my femininity. It is a stone for psychological protection and reduces stress. Other crystals placed on the artwork were turquoise, connecting to Serapis Bey and Malachite, for the heart and throat communication with Brigid.

Francine placed my depiction upon a gold seed of life symbol, the carnelian gracing its edges and representing my understanding of the mysteries. Saint Germaine is shown overseeing my spiritual mastery, and Serapis Bey stands watch as I expand in love and light. Serapis Bey is my connection, along with Hathor (her symbol found in the necklace), to the influence of music, sound and vibrational healing. Hathor is the goddess of beauty, music and dance. I have lived many lives as a Priestess and High Priestess, and have close ties with Sirius, Lyra and the Pleiades. Francine also saw me in many lives exploring dance, spiritual culture and all things transcendent, with an incredible ability to hold, process and expand in love and mental understanding, able to transmute the energies of the people around me.

The symbols continued to reveal themselves and leave me awestruck in their wake. Another aspect of the painting was a huge Stag standing beside me, my hand resting on his head. As someone who follows the signs of nature, I can honestly say I had never really looked up the spiritual or symbolic meaning of the Stag, and when it did, it revealed yet another powerful revelation.

The Stag symbolises walking in harmony with the earth, to celebrate the path of spirit, to ponder the meaning of life, and participate in a personal quest for the White Stag. Scott King, in his exceptional book *Animal Messenger*, describes the symbolic meaning of the stag, which is to participate in the Quest for the Holy Grail. When we participate in the quest, though, what is it that we are truly looking for? The answer is, of course, as Scott suggests, our inner self. In Celtic mythology, the White Stag often appears as an omen indicating the nearness of the other world. It can also appear as a warning, or as motivation to a quest for knowledge. The White Stag often appeared in the Arthurian myths and stories, sending the knights on adventures, emerging from the mists, and challenging them to track deep into the forest.[2]

Scott continues to explain that when we pursue the White Stag, the chase may lead us out into the world, daring us to take risks and try new things. It can lead us to other realms and dimensions, encouraging us to explore spirit, past lives and our higher selves, but generally it guides us into the underworld. When we symbolically follow the stag, we are being invited to journey deep within our consciousness where we are ultimately left to contemplate life and seek the wisdom of our innocence. Energetically, the White Stag is seen as being dark, nurturing and contemplative. Traditionally, to quest for the White Stag is to seek and trust the answers found deep within our inner knowing, before we consider the advice given to us by well-meaning others.

The White Stag is, in fact a representation of our own soul with the hunt proving to be a vital and necessary lesson in self-discovery. The fate of the White Stag is symbolic of the evolutionary passage of the soul, the developmental journey of growth experienced when one battles change on all planes of awareness. The mythical knight seeking to evolve, stalking his own perceptions, attracting his values, shadows and purpose, follows the stag deep into the forest with steadfast intent, motivation and resolve, his mindset firmly on the task at hand. Impeccable in his quest, the knight displays resolute endurance, legitimacy, courage and commitment.

Woven deeply into the stories of King Arthur and Camelot, the brave Knights of the Round Table, the Holy Grail, Excalibur and the red deer, the embodiment of the White Stag protects us as we embark on quests that will see us secure our sacred self. Its dreaming leads us on adventures that will offer many tests, obstacles and challenges to see us champion our own sacred cause, and face personal demons, emerging as a stronger, braver, wiser individual.[2]

The pieces to the puzzle began to seem to me like sacred codes and keys of the ancient symbols speaking clearly through the paint. It has been suggested that symbols such as the Holy Grail, Excalibur, King Arthur, and Albion are codes within the matrix of life, the once and future king, like a coded time capsule waiting to be opened. These templates and stories are full of triggers and codices that are huge awakeners for many on the planet right now, and which are always assisting with the triggering and opening of our consciousness.

These metaphors, stories, or historical facts brought to life, however, you see it, are like codes that speak to our soul, and higher self. Words such as the Knights of the Round Table for example are extremely profound as they evoke symbols of the flower of life, balance, and equality for all men. And these triggers are mostly found in story, art, film, music and books to awaken the dream within. Many of us have a feeling of awe and wonder around the symbols, no matter what our history or background.[3]

It is important to note here that in no way do I necessarily use this information to build some notion that I am what she saw, or that I am more important, or more special than anyone else. For me, the significance of the painting is that it points the way. It gathers the signs, symbols and information needed to confirm my path, and inspires me to continue on my own journey and Quest. The truth is, for many weeks prior to truly understanding all the signposts within this painting, I actually struggled to look at it. I couldn't see myself in it at all. The fact that I rolled it up, not even sure I would hang it, told me a few things. One, I had no idea of the significance of the embedded meanings, and two I didn't come close to thinking that the woman depicted holding that sword was me. And, I probably didn't feel worthy to embody its message.

When I finally did understand, I was humbled and sobered by the direction these symbols were pointing. I understood fully that I had to do what had always been asked of me: trust, walk the journey and communicate it to others. They can then make of it whatever they choose. If it inspires and uplifts you then I am humbled. If not, I understand that the symbols embedded in this story are not the signposts for your journey. And that is perfect. I do believe though, that these ancient signposts are pointing and asking the descendants of their origin to awaken, stand together, and allow their magical power to transform us into our highest potential.

They are asking us to seek the Grail and our highest potential and true self, to follow the path of the White Stag and the Scared Quest that is within, to stand for equality of all people sitting at the round table of life, and to balance the sword Excalibur, Truth, and the power of love. Was I truly being asked, in living reality, to hold and wield Excalibur? Was it all just symbolic, or was there more to it? In the end I put it down to a really impressive story and let it all go as a special experience.

I could finally see the importance of leaning into these symbols, and embodying them in one way or another, to continue expressing, through my own art, these codes, symbols and signposts for others to be awakened or inspired by. What task would I be asked to achieve now? The next piece of the puzzle and the Blacksmith blew my mind.

18

THE BLACKSMITH

"Miracles are both beginnings and endings, and so they alter the temporal order. They are always affirmations of rebirth, which seem to go back, but really go forward. They undo the past in the present, and thus release the future."

- A COURSE IN MIRACLES [1]

My journey with the blacksmith began almost 10 years ago, when I emailed him to ask to have my first sword forged. Because the swords are handmade, they are true works of art, and I am very proud to own one. The next part of this story made me wonder how far back the dots to this journey had started. Did I have control over my destiny at all, or was I just a cork bobbing in the universal sea, following crumbs I didn't even know were crumbs in the first place. If I hadn't moved to Glenmore Park in 2008 and flipped through a newspaper to see the advertisement that my dance teacher had published in a local Gazette, I would never have known the Tribal Belly Dancing group existed.

I wouldn't have joined, journeyed, and met the blacksmith along the way. In the last 10 years, I have had a couple of different swords forged, and we see each other at festivals and events on a regular basis. The blacksmith's swords are a beloved part of the tribal, traditional, and re-enactment communities, and he creates swords and other weapons for all sorts of people with all sort of historical and performance arts inter-ests.

The fact that I made it to dance at the 2019 Newcastle Belly Dance Festival was a miracle, as I had been incredibly busy the year before with my father's cancer, illness, death and completion of his estate. I had barely danced all year. This was so unusual for me as Tuesday night dance was an important part of my mental, physical, and emotional health. But this year I was tired, and I could barely drag myself to class, let alone prepare for a major performance. With about eight weeks to go before the event, my teacher and I chatted, and I decided it was time to commit, and just get myself back to class. One class under my belt, completely exhausted but fulfilled, I decided that I could get myself up to speed in the short time we had left to prepare for the festival.

The last day of the festival saw me browsing the tribal belly dance bizarre, a place where you could get lost down a rabbit hole of beautiful things, items, clothing, colourful outfits, belts, coins, jewels and, yes, swords. Here was the blacksmith at the back of the room with his array of swords sitting on his table ready for sale. I spent quite some time chatting with a couple of ladies from the group who had been bitten by the sword bug and felt ready to buy their own. After a few laughs, trying various styles, the two ladies chose their new shiny friends, the blacksmith making a joke that one of the ladies should call her sword (as all good swords need a name you know) Edward!

"You should name your sword after my sixth Generation Grandfa-ther! His name is Sir Edward Field Esquire," he exclaimed with a huge smile on his face and a cheeky glint in his eye that I like to think only a good sword maker could conjure.

"I love it," I said

As much as this was a very funny moment, this wasn't the message that Edward Field and the ancestors were trying to communicate. I just didn't hear them at the time. How frustrating it must be for all those on the other side of the veil desperately arranging and guiding, pulling strings and whispering in our ears, only for us to mostly miss the message! I imagine their invisible foreheads must be red from slapping them so many times.

"Well then, my dear friend," I said to my friend who had just purchased her new sword, "I think you have a name for your new baby!"

"I think I do!"

She was very impressed and excited, and that was where the interaction ended. Nothing significant at all. I said my goodbyes to my silver-bearded friend, noted how nice it was to see him, and began to make my way back to Sydney. With a few hours' drive ahead of me I was keen to get on the road and home again before the terrible Sunday afternoon traffic that invariably chokes the M1 between Newcastle and the city.

At home, I was surprised when Steve suggested we watch something on Netflix. We didn't watch much television and it wasn't how we would usually spend a Sunday night. And so, I begrudgingly scrolled through the endless movies and series that seemed to have nothing to offer me whatsoever. Until I flashed past the series called Merlin. I knew almost nothing about Merlin and was surprised to see that the show began to tell the tale of Merlin and King Arthur. My husband, initially not impressed with my choice, sat down to begin watching the series with me, and from the very first episode I was hooked.

I literally journeyed through the story stumbling over connections that reflected back into my life and what I was going through, and it started to get a little freaky. At this point I was thoroughly enjoying the story of Merlin, a quirky man who becomes a dear and loyal friend to King Arthur, and their quest to bring peace to Camelot. I can't recall the exact moment I was confronted by Excalibur in the story line, though I do recall feeling the hair on the back of my neck stand to attention as Merlin journeyed down to see the 'all wise and all knowing' Dragon below Camelot to forge Excalibur, the most mystical and powerful sword known in history. For the first time since I saw my painting, I began to feel the pieces fall into place, and understand that there might be more to the reason why Francine felt called to paint me as a woman from the Arthurian age, holding none other than Excalibur. But what?

A few days after I saw the scenes in Merlin of Excalibur being magically forged by the Ancient Dragon of the Druids, I had this prompting begin. The voice softly said, "Angela, call the sword maker and ask him to forge Excalibur."

I could hear this voice, but I didn't want to. I blew off the experience by saying to myself, "Angela, it is nice that you have been painted with Excalibur, quite a lovely privilege, but it's just a painting. Leave it there. Who do you think you are?" But for days this little voice kept going around and around in my mind. It would pop into my head at the strangest moments, and as the journey with Merlin continued, I could ignore it no more. Okay! Fine! I will text him, at least then when he says "no, go get a life Angela," I can sleep at night and whoever is annoying me with this silly idea will stop because I did what they asked.

So, I wrote a short text that read: "Hey, it was so nice to see you the other week at Newcastle! Just wondering, any chance you could forge me Excalibur LOL?" (With a few laughing emojis and crazy faces to ensure that if he thought I was crazy I could buffer with, "Just joking!") Silence for a day or so.

Then a message came back. "Hi Angela, yes always nice to see you. And no." (Shocked emoji face). Totally stumped I thought, hmm ok, well that is that then. So texted back, "Ok no worries LOL (crazy faces and laughing) All good, thanks anyway."

Another text came back. "Angela, there are many online, you can order them all over. Not worth the work it would take when you can get them around. But why do you want one?"

Ok so here was my chance to really make him think I was crazy. I pondered my next response. "Well it is a bit of a long story, it is for a monument project that I have been working on, that I think, not sure why, but think Excalibur may be a part of it."

"Okay, well how about you call me tomorrow and explain," he replied.

"Sounds good," I said. "No problem, I will call you tomorrow. Talk then."

And so, we had made a date for me to explain as best I could this crazy story and see where the chips fell. That night I decided to do a little more research on Excalibur. I wondered what symbolic significance it held in history, and if there was there any deeper meaning beyond the usual mystical portrayals most people knew.

I looked up Excalibur's symbolic meaning, and the first site that popped up on my screen said, 'British sovereignty.' I sat with my heart in my mouth. I had no idea that was what it meant, and here I was in a painting, created by someone who knew nothing of me, standing on the canvas holding the symbol of British sovereignty. And what may we ask is most important to the First Nations people? Sovereignty. I felt a surge of responsibility as timelines collapsed, ancient myths and the present-day merged into one and stared me in the face. I went to bed that night, my head spinning in anticipation of what might come of the call with the blacksmith.

The next morning, I got up made my coffee and prepared myself for the call. I explained that my story technically started when I was about 17 years old, after my father received a package in the mail from a lady named Valda Shrimpton. I explained how she had spent many years of her life studying the family tree, and followed the line from our First and Second fleet ancestors, Mary Davis Bishop and Richard Shrimpton, to my father. She had simply asked my father to help complete the tree by adding his family and any other information he might have to add to the research.

I told him how Valda's simple request had improbably expanded to the possibility of creating a monument of peace between First Nations people and First Settlers descendants at Wilberforce, and ultimately how the journey had now led me to him. By this time, an hour or so had passed, and the sword-smith and his wife sat quietly listening to my tale, not really giving me any feedback at first. I got to what I felt was the most I could tell them in the time we had, and I stopped, took a breath and said, "well that sums up the short version of the long story, what do you think?"

"Thank you for sharing that story, it truly is amazing," he said.

"My wife and I are sitting here with tears in our eyes to be honest. I am dumb struck, and you are not going to believe what I am about to tell you!"

My eyes widened. "What is it?"

"So, Angela, what you need to know is that I am a sixth-generation blacksmith, and the family lineage goes right back to England. My ancestor came on the Second Fleet, his name was Edward Field. Edward came to this country on the exact same ship your ancestor Richard came on, the Scarborough! They probably sat together, for months on end in that boat, chained side by side. He survived that voyage, and ended up being one of the first land holders in the Hawkesbury, just like Richard!"[2]

The sword maker's ancestor Edward had a brother named William Field who arrived on the First Fleet ship, the Friendship. He is buried in Wilberforce Cemetery (Cathy & Nichols McHardy. 2003 *Sacred to the memory: A Study of Wilberforce Cemetery*. Hawkesbury City Council) and Edward Field is buried just a stone's throw away in Castlereagh. Edward Field was enlisted as a Private in the 102nd Regiment of the New South Wales Corps, on 27 July 1789, some seven weeks after its formation. He arrived in the Colony of New South Wales on the Scarborough, along with Richard Shrimpton, on 28 June 1790. On 13 December 1794 Edward, along with a number of other 'lesser ranks,' received a grant of 25 acres on the west side of Iron Cove Creek, the area that is now Five Dock. That grant, which would have been heavily timbered at that time and quite poor-quality farmland, was subsequently revoked, and on 30 June 1803, Edward received a grant of 100 acres of land at Castlereagh in its place.[3]

He received a further grant of 100 acres at upper Cranbrook (now submerged as part of the Nepean Lakes complex) on 10 May 1809. On 8 August 1801, he was granted his discharge from the New South Wales Corps. In addition to farming, he was renowned for his skills as a blacksmith. In particular, he is recorded as having provided blacksmithing services to William Cox's team, which constructed the first road over the Blue Mountains.

So, it turned out that I was talking to a Second Fleet descendant, whose ancestor was also one of the earliest blacksmiths in the country, one of the first men to make metal items of all kinds, even for the explorers travelling across the Blue Mountains. We had ancestors who had come to Australia on the very same ship, surviving horrendous conditions that had killed many others, and who both lived, farmed and died in the Hawkesbury.

The sword-smith finished his part of the story by saying: "There is no one else to make your Excalibur. If it is time to ensure that Sovereignty is returned to the Original people of this country, then as a sixth-generation ancestor of the Second Fleet, and sixth generation blacksmith, I will be the one to make it. And I don't even know why, but yes, I will make it for you."

Within a week or so we met in Windsor, not too far from Wilberforce, in the oldest pub in Australia, the Macquarie Arms, a place where our ancestors possibly drank, sat and worked together in this new world they were all creating. Like a mythical tale, we now had a sixth-generation ancestor forging Excalibur, a symbol of power, love and sovereignty. I would indeed, as prophetically shown in a painting by someone who didn't know me, soon hold this great symbol. I was reminded of what Merlin's mentor, the ancient dragon, had said when Arthur died: "Take heart Merlin, Arthur is the Once and Future King. Arthur will arise again when Albion needs him most."

That night, after a mind boggling day (as my dad would say), I watched the last couple of episodes of the Merlin series, sobbing through the final scenes as Arthur died in Merlin's arms. The word Albion, which I had heard a hundred times in the series, truly rang a bell now. Albion, I thought to myself. What is this Albion, and why were Arthur and Merlin trying to create it? Just as I was about to retire for the night, I searched the word "Albion."

A site popped up on the search as number one, and it read: "Indeed, if Arthur Phillip's personal dream for the new colony had been realised, we might now be living in a sort of enlightenment utopia called Albion, using the name derived by Phillip from the foundational myth of England."[4]

Arthur Phillip came from England, but how did this myth make any sense in the context of the establishment of the colony at Sydney Cove? Until then, I'd had no idea what Albion even was, and knew absolutely nothing of our First Governor. But I was about to meet and get to know him really well. As I lay in bed reading and re-reading the words to make sure I hadn't made it up or mistaken it, I cried. I actually sobbed. My mind cracked open, and I lay there that night wondering where the heck this rabbit hole was leading me. Was I going completely mad?

Albion it seems was the next piece of the puzzle.

19

THE GOVERNOR

"Nothing is more powerful than an idea whose time has come."

- VICTOR HUGO

Michael Pembroke had three objectives in writing his book *Arthur Phillip: Sailor, Mercenary, Governor, Spy*. He wanted to convey something of Phillip's elusive character, highlight his career in the Royal Navy and bring to life the Georgian society in which he lived and died. As I typed the word 'Albion' into an online search I was dumbfounded by the information that Pembroke revealed to me.[1] I had no prior knowledge or understanding of Albion's meaning and had only just been introduced to it through the mythical story of Merlin.

It quickly became clear to me that I also knew very little about the foundations of this country. Even after seemingly endless history classes at school, I had barely covered the basics of colonial society. I knew nothing at all about the desires and motivations of those who played integral parts in leading that society.

No matter how the story is conveyed in history classes, it is impossible to escape the ultimate truth that our ancestors' arrival here and the way it was handled by not only the government of the time, but the settlers themselves, resulted in the tragic and needless devastation of the first people and their culture, leading to generations of displacement, pain and suffering. What Pembroke's revelations gave me was an alternative perspective on Arthur Philip. Pembroke tells of Phillip's extraordinary idealism, which was inspired by the greatest foundational myth of Britain. Pembroke helped me to look through the eyes of a man travelling on a ship as the very first Governor and leader of what he and his superiors considered to be a new land, thousands of miles away from all they knew and all they loved. I am in no way saying this to minimise the impact of Phillip's arrival in this land we now know as Australia. But it helps me to see from a point of compassion, this one side of the coin, which in turn might help me apply that same compassion to the stories of my ancestors and the role they played in the colonisation of this country.

Arthur Phillip was born in London in October 1738 during the reign of Britain's last foreign-born monarch, George II. After receiving his commission as Governor of New South Wales on 12 October 1786, he spent the next few months, until May 1787, deep in preparations for the journey. Arthur was deeply concerned to make the endeavour a success, and all his focus was on the fit out of ships, and the procurement and storage of food, medicine, clothing and building supplies for both the trip and first years of settlement.[2]

By Pembroke's account, garnered from his considerable research, Phillip's main concern was to maintain the health of the convicts and marines on board. This was a matter of deep professional pride for Phillip, but there was much more to it. Pembroke explains that Phillip's resolve was as much due to his humanity, as it was to his professional understanding of the magnitude of the journey ahead, and all that was at stake. Phillip took his anxieties directly to the Home Secretary, Lord Sydney, in March 1787 after many months of frustration, and requested assistance, pointing out that the garrison and convicts were being sent to "the extremity of the globe as if being sent to America, merely a six week passage." Phillip stressed that he had repeatedly pointed out the consequences of so many men and women being crowded on board such small ships for the duration of a monumental voyage.[3]

A highly experienced seaman, Phillip was well aware of the sickness and disease so often experienced on arduous journeys and he knew the convicts who were to be confined below deck would be the most vulnerable. Exasperated, he demanded the fulfilment of orders for stores, implements, medicines, and supplies. Once landed and living in the experimental settlement of New South Wales, Phillip was empowered to release convicts and grant land as rewards for good conduct and disposition. Augustus Alt was appointed as surveyor of lands to administer these grants.

Pembroke wrote that it was hoped the convicts would be improved and reformed, the men would become farmers, the women would raise children, and the land would be settled. Infused by a utopian concept of a simple society without money, the goal was to rebirth convict men and women through the hardships of physical labour and farming in the new world. Philanthropic in his nature and characterised by an enlightened benevolence for his time, Phillip assumed the best, not the worst. He shared with others his intention to persuade a few of the Aborigines to settle near the colony, so they could be supplied with everything required to "civilise" them. His hope was to impress them, and give a high opinion of "their new guests." Significantly, when it came to homicide, Phillip regarded the life of an Aboriginal man as the equal of any Englishman and told the members of the colony that "any man who takes the life of a native will be put on trial as if you killed one of the garrison. This appears to me not only just, but good policy."[4]

Looking back through the lens of history, we can see how damaging even the best of British intentions were. For the people already living in the newly proclaimed colony of NSW, and throughout the rest of the land, did not ask to be civilised, but to remain free, with sovereignty, raising families and practising their culture as they had done for tens of thousands of years before the arrival of the First Fleet. It was not for the British to civilise them, but to respect and honour their way of life and balance.

But looking at another side of the coin, we can see that in the context of the society that Arthur Phillip had come from, he was somewhat of a visionary, and was a humanitarian at heart. I also learned from Pembroke's book that Phillip was firmly opposed to slavery and supported the antislavery campaigns of William Wilberforce. He had seen the worst of the Portuguese and Dutch slaving practices in Brazil and Cape Town, and was staunch in his stance against the introduction of slavery to the colony of New South Wales. "There can be no slavery in a free land, and consequently no slaves," Phillip is quoted as saying.

It was in this revelation that I saw another layer, the collapsing of the timelines from ancient to present, and a connection to the people and events of 230 years ago. I can feel, see, and hear, the presence of men such as Wilberforce and Phillip standing behind me, and wishing for this story to be told through the eyes of the past with the wisdom of the future. Benevolence aside, Arthur Phillip had his own grand designs for the colony. He wanted it to be called Albion, the ancient name for Britain. That name conjures the ancient stories of King Arthur, Merlin, the Round Table, the Holy Grail, and Excalibur, and brings them into alignment with Phillip's place and time. The symbolism cries out once more to the descendants of this bloodline, who feel this myth within their DNA. It is literally begging us to begin the Quest to find our greatest potential.

How many of us have been taught that Arthur Phillip, the first Governor of this country, wanted to nam the settlement Albion? How many of us have learned the significance and symbolism of that name? For many of us, this part of our history has been lost, and it is time that we learn that we too have an ancient myth that shapes us. It is time to hear the voice of our ancient ancestors who have fought this battle before and foretold the rising again of the energy of Arthur, with Arthur being a symbol of the consciousness of hope, love, unconditional peace and personal right to sovereignty.

The stories of Albion's foundation are found in The Faerie Queene (1596). The poet Edmond Spencer said that the name Albion was bestowed in honour of an ancestral giant who conquered the British Isles.

According to legend, Albion founded the island country that was to become Britain before he was killed by Hercules. Albion's descendants continued to inhabit the island until Brutus of Troy vanquished them, more than 1000 years before the Roman invasion. The huge white horses inscribed on the chalk hills of southern England are said to be traces of that era.

I don't know why, but my awareness of the deep significance of Albion, its energy in our country's history, and its silent presence within our DNA, brings me to tears. Every time I'm confronted with this story of our ancient past and what we are being called to do, I am left in awe and wonder. Some would say that Albion is built on myth alone, and they might be right. But there is something about the stories that have been passed down age to age, like a treasure waiting to be found, a trigger of something we have long forgotten, that it is time to again remember.

Among Phillip's influential patrons, Lord Sydney was one to whom he owed the most. Pembroke's research showed that Phillip gained Sydney's entire confidence as they worked together through the winter and early spring months, preparing for the journey of the First Fleet. Perhaps Phillip felt compelled to honour his friend in the new settlement's name, and let go of his initial desire for Albion. But with all this talk about naming the land, and the mythical significance of Albion, we risk missing the key point. The area chosen for the new settlement already had a name, if only someone had thought to ask what it was, and to honour it.

At this point, I wish to make it clear that it is not my desire to idealise the 18th Century British way of thinking, or imply that Australia should have developed into a place more like Albion. I tell the story in the way that I do to enliven the symbols and trigger the memory within you that there is more to us, particularly those of us who believe the story that we are the descendants of convicts only. We too have distant and ancient beginnings that lie deep within us and create a potential and a destiny that is just waiting to be fulfilled.

I have heard it said that our ancestors were sent here as the trash of

British society, the lowest of the low, the criminals and thieves of the British world. But it is kinder to remember that many of these people came from a society that was already struggling, where people were suffering under the pressure of a system that was not based on humanitarian policies. Of course, there were hardened criminals who came to Australia as convicts, but so many, including my ancestors, had to steal basic items and foods for the purpose of survival alone.

Two of my ancestors, Mary Davis Bishop and Richard Shrimpton, had dark moments in their lives when they thought they would hang for their crimes. They were given a reprieve, only to be forced to participate in one of history's biggest social experiments, which saw a group of convicts and their captors sent to the other side of the world to begin a whole new society, some of them with nothing more than the rags on their bodies when they arrived on the ships, like skeletal ghosts, from 1788 onwards.

Phillip considered himself a servant to the cause of humanity, and he tried to earn the affection of the Aborigines, encouraging everyone to live in harmony and kindness. According to Pembroke, Phillip's approach was gentler than that of Cook and Lapérouse, who regarded the Aborigines as malevolent savages to be avoided.[4]

But while genuinely wishing to befriend the Aboriginals, Phillip and the settlers were sadly blind to the fact that they were invaders. They thought of themselves as enlightened, tolerant and chivalrous citizens of the British Empire, bringing the virtues of British civilisation to the world. And they viewed the Aborigines through the eyes of the prevailing European misconceptions and condescension. Instructed to achieve amity and kindness with the original inhabitants, and refrain from pillage or harm, the colonists nevertheless appropriated and ruined Aboriginal hunting and fishing grounds. Initially, there was no violent racist terror. But the generalised racist terror of lands taken, food stocks destroyed and an assumption that assimilation and civilisation were the best ways forward, was instigated from the start.

Phillip's dream of peaceful coexistence did not come to fruition, even though in the first few days of their arrival, convicts and marines had danced and jigged on the beach with the curious and good-natured natives. Phillip had approached the Aboriginal people with open arms, forbidding any one to shoot, and handed out gifts, beads, mirrors and bright cloths.

Whatever Phillip's intentions, it all went wrong. When he finally left the shores of New South Wales, a seriously ill man in excruciating pain, to return to England, Aboriginals had been kidnapped, people on both sides had been killed and injured, so many had died from illnesses they had no resistance to, and animosity and grievances were growing on both sides. The stage was being set for the worse that was to come. With our modern knowledge, attitudes and the benefit of hindsight, it can be difficult to acknowledge, that while many atrocities were committed out of greed, malice and sheer hatred, other damaging actions were committed with good intentions. It's hard to swallow, and doesn't make any of those actions right, but it can give a more rounded understanding of our history, a perspective from two different sides of the coin.

And perhaps it can help us to understand the significance of the chance we have now, to look back with wisdom and make conscious choices to help heal the wounds of our past, and actively seek to repair the damage done. We have the opportunity now to evolve our humanity in such a way that in another 250 years our descendants will look back at this time as a pivotal moment where our generation consciously took a quantum leap to transform our thinking forever. They will probably wonder why it took us so long to get to this point and make the required changes, just as we do when we look back at the women's suffrage movement and the emancipation of slaves in America. It is up to us now, to not let it take any longer. And so as the Queen requested, I wrote the Governor General.

The Governor General His Excellency, Hon Sir David Hurley
Government House Dunrossil Drive
Yarralumla ACT 2600

(Also sent to The Queen of England)

Your Excellency,

My name is Angela Sciberras (nee Shrimpton) and this is one of
many letters I have taken the time to write to both the previous Governor General and Her Majesty in the past year. I am honoured to say
that each and every letter has been replied to with sincerity, and I live
in hope that these new words will be received with an open heart and
mind.

Firstly, I congratulate you on your recent appointment as Her
Majesty's Governor General of Australia. I humbly admit that your acceptance speech brought many a tear to my eye in the hope that you
would be the one we have been waiting for to assist in this great task
that I now often call Project Excalibur. It would be an honour personally deliver from Buckingham Palace "The Queen's Letter," and to hence
transport this precious work of paper, pen, power, peace and privilege
to the people of this nation of Australia.

Such a simple act, mere paper, ink and love in action. I thank you for
at minimum hearing my request, that even in the asking, not knowing
whether it can indeed be done, leaves it magnificent. This day I write
you from the deepest and oldest place of what I now come to realise is
my ancestral myth. A myth so moving, and so transformational I must
share it with you. This story I understand is new to you, and so I invite
you to read the included letters from the past to gain a full understanding of this project and how it has developed over many years of my life.
This letter pertains to just a tiny snippet of the total journey of over 25
years.

In the time since my last letter, the Queen requested that I seek
council with our Australian Governor General, and Commander /

Prime Minister, and since this time much has fallen into place and in some ways brought me to my knees in its beauty. It has been very challenging to be taken seriously by such people as our Prime Minister, and Governor General, and I deeply hope that it may be possible to be invited for a meeting as soon as possible to discuss in full my great task.

Your Excellency, when I witnessed your swearing in ceremony I was moved to my core as I heard you describe your objectives in office to support our communities, particularly Aboriginal Australia and our peaceful unfoldment. What was even more astounding was to hear you, our new Governor General, give the Welcome to Country in traditional Aboriginal First Nations language. I'm sure this was a first in our nation's history and had me in tears of joy. Thank you for such a profound course of action that would have taken much courage.

Your Excellency, I felt a real urgency to let you know what has been unfolding. I feel that the time is now to move forward with 2020 being the 250-year anniversary of Cook's circumnavigation of Australia, which triggered the colonisation of our country. What I am about to say may sound impossible to some, but I assure you it is all true, and even after all the amazing synchronicities, what comes next proves to be truly divine in nature. There is a woman, who is a talented artist. Her skill however is not just in wielding paint but bringing to life the soul essence of a person, their highest potential in life. I humbly commissioned the artist to complete my portrait. We had a conversation, and she went off to paint.

I honestly told her nothing of my journey, not even what I do for work. Even these letters and my aims remained silent to her. I was later perplexed to find she had painted me dressed like a woman from the time of King Arthur, and the Knights of the Round Table, holding what she called 'Excalibur.'

A week or so after receiving this painting, I left it rolled up in my spare room as I truly could not see how I was connected to this depiction. The art didn't really make any sense to me. In honest truth I knew very little of the legends of King Arthur and all the astounding symbolism they hold. I feel quite embarrassed to say how little I truly knew about my own ancestral legend. It was a lovely thought that someone would paint or see me in such a way knowing nothing of me. Excalibur goes down in history and myth as the sword of truth, valour, power, and pure heart.

A week or so later I sent a message to someone I have known for quite a few years, but only as someone who created handmade swords for performers and enactments. I contacted him almost as a laugh to see if he would be so inclined to forge me a replica of Excalibur. He initially said no. I assumed he thought I wanted one for my wall, so told him it would be for a symbolic monument, and I would need to explain. I called him on Saturday 13 July at 2pm and explained this story. I completed what is, as you can see, a long explanation.

He laughed and said, "Angela you are not going to believe what I am about to say."

A 6th Generation Blacksmith. He has two Ancestors that came to Australia on First and Second Fleet ships. Edward Field, Second Fleet arrived on the Scarborough, the very same ship my ancestor Richard Shrimpton arrived on. He was a Blacksmith and Soldier. Edward Field is quite famous in our area and NSW as one of, if not the first Blacksmith in the Hawkesbury, and one of the first landowners. He did work for the explorers who discovered the path across the Blue Mountains and served the community my ancestors began in this country. They most probably knew each other well from ship to death. This man is buried within minutes of Wilberforce Cemetery at Castlereagh.

When he told me this information, we were both in tears, he wishing to be a part of this journey. Just when one considers that matters could not become more astounding, they did. In the last few days what I have learned is that I have never really connected with my British dreaming. Many of us here haven't. We continue to tell the tales of the convict, forgetting the legends from which we come and can aspire to, the British legends and history that inspires and mystifies. As I am sure you know well, King Arthur of Avalon was the 'Once and Future King,' who led the Knights of the Round Table, a table that was created to show that there is no-one greater than another on a round table. His quest was to bring peace to all the United Kingdoms, all people, of all kinds. His dream was to create 'Albion.'

I realise now your Excellency this is my real end. Albion. You would remember our first Governor General Arthur Phillip? Well in my research it seems that many historians place him as a kind man, who had a vision for Australia, and dreamed of creating a place of peace and democracy. He felt that all people were equal, didn't believe in slavery, and wished for all men and women to have the same rights no matter their race, or place in society. Well he too believed in the legend of King Arthur, so much so that he actually originally named Sydney, 'New Albion.' Albion, as you know, in the oldest language, is the name for Britain.

What this tells me is how deeply this legend runs in the dreaming of British people, of your lineage and that ultimately even in my own history and the many here in Australia. This magical story of King Arthur and the Knights of the Round Table, and so much more is a part of the fabric of what it is to be most proud of our British roots and ancestry. The truth is, our ancestors came here to create the New Albion, a beautiful vision that we can still achieve someday.

The legend says that Arthur was the 'Once and Future King,' and that one day, when Britain most needs him, he will arise again. How amazing would it be, to connect our own beautiful dreaming, to this process? Let the symbolism of hope and peace run as deep as our British lineage can go, back to one of the most inspiring times on earth. Our Commander and Prime Minister has commissioned the Endeavour Replica to travel around this country next year to commemorate the 250-year anniversary of Captain Cook's circumnavigation of Australia. Imagine travelling to Avalon with this newly forged Excalibur, made by the descendant of the first blacksmith of our lands. Blessing it in the waters of Avalon and the energies of this sacred time, most divine and filled with hope. Imagine how powerful it would be, to then travel to London to collect the letters from the Queen, letters filled with the hope of New Albion, lasting bringing it back here. Image what a story we could leave for generations to tell in years to come.

I feel God / Conscience has set before me Three Great Objects:

1) A Sandstone Stone Circle. This will be a joint creation for the purpose of recognition and reconciliation. This small parcel of land (The Wesleyan Section) is adjacent to the significant Wilberforce Cemetery, and is marked 'Crown Land.' It will also stand as an act of grace in naming all unmarked graves in this significant cemetery, including my own ancestor Richard Shrimpton.

Wilberforce Cemetery is of great national significance with a rich and rare evidence of Australia's earliest ex-convict pioneer society. I have been given permission by Hawkesbury Council to do the above work, though I feel it weigh heavily on my mind and heart, to create a much deeper act of significance. Wilberforce is also an area of significant beginnings of early Australian settlement, and more importantly is in the region of one of the first sites/areas of commissioned native slaughters in the country's history. This makes the area one of the most significant places in modern Australian history in terms of colonial settlement. It is where it all started, and it is my hope you will see the vision laid upon my heart, as a most powerful extension and of coming full circle. It is my deep hope that you can see with me the power we have in our hands to create something together as Crown, First Nations and First Settler descendants. I have personally witnessed in the early stages of the development of this project the coming together and embracing of direct descendants of both First Nations and ex-convict, free settler people, and it is beyond moving to say the very least.

2) The Action of Greater Significance I seek is to hand this Crown Land, now named The Wesleyan Section back to the Traditional Owners, with your seal of approval and support, where, henceforth will stand a memorial and sacred place of remembrance, reconciliation, and unity. The days of creating monuments and gardens in the name of peace, with the belief that such a token act be enough to show sincerity, are over. It is time for a powerful act, from one descendant to another. A powerful symbol of the now genuine nature of our plan to reconcile our past for a peaceful, prosperous future for all Australians.

3) Heartfelt apology and acknowledgement from the Crown. I

humbly request a letter and expression of the Crown's support of the reconciliation between our people, and the extension of a vision of a prosperous path ahead. I humbly request within this historical document the expression of profound regret and apology. The honouring of the Indigenous people of this land and regret for the suffering and loss of those Indigenous, and non-Indigenous.

This is not a request for admittance of fault, but an act of love and reconciliation, as part of the natural healing process of the injustices of the past for a more prosperous present. This, a moral and ethical act, an act of good conscience and demonstration of respect of all humanity, with the overall goal of restoring dignity and sound harmony. I believe in Her Majesty and her supreme love and power, and what it has taken to be one of the greatest Monarchs of all time, and in what God entrusted in her all those years ago. May forgiveness set the ancestors, and our generations to come, free. Arthur was not just a King, he is and was the once and future king, allow us to take heart, for it is foretold that when Albion's need is greatest, Arthur will rise again. Allow the ancient myth of the first settlers of this country to arise to heal the hearts of the many as we connect to our greatest potential as British ancestors, the New Albion that King Arthur and Arthur Phillip stood for. For the sweetest words ever to hear are not "I'm sorry," but "I forgive you."

Your Excellency, I pray that you may be the Governor General who will pick up where Governor General Arthur Phillip left off. That you may be the Governor General who will complete his great task of bringing lasting peace to our people by stepping into the greatest myth of hope of all time. You will see in the book *Arthur Philip: Sailor, Mercenary, Governor, Spy* written by Michael Pembroke that Arthur Phillip embodied the ideal of Australia as the optimistic and well-intentioned project of the British Enlightenment. Pembroke portrays the commander of the First Fleet and first governor of New South Wales as more than just a skilled navigator. For him, Arthur Phillip was a wise and (for the times) humane leader of men, a visionary genuinely wanting to create a better society.

Arise Sir David Hurley, 27th Governor General of Australia. Please help me raise the attention of our Commander and Chief to complete this most beautiful task. Her Majesty has sent me to you. I believe she now awaits your advice and communication, but we need the guidance of our Prime Minister to do so.

May the spirit of Albion rise once more within us all. For our story has not ended, there is still so much to come. Let Australia truly reveal herself. You are right, she is far from a finished product.

"Australia is still revealing itself to us. We oughtn't to close off possibilities by declaring too early what we have already become."
— David Malouf

Sincerely,
Angela Sciberras 1 August 2019

20

FORGIVEN

*"Forgiveness is the fragrance that the violet sheds on the heel that has
crushed it."*

- MARK TWAIN

Sitting in a coffee shop in Kurrajong, the place where my First Fleet
ancestor Mary lived at the end of her life with her daughter Charlotte,
I felt a strange compulsion to research slaughters in the Hawkesbury.
That search led me to Richmond Hill. We drove the short distance
down the mountain towards what is now a place called St John of God,
where a memorial garden commemorates the Dharug people of Richmond and the Hawkesbury. The site commemorates the 1795 Battle of
Richmond Hill, where Dharug people fought to defend their lands from
invasion.

Even as a descendent of Hawkesbury settlers and First and Second
Fleet convicts, even though I had in the past attended St John of God,
even though I had lived in Kurrajong and Richmond for quite a few
years, I had never heard about the battle on this land. We arrived at the
memorial and I walked over to a huge sign over looking a pile of river

stones. It was then I realised this place looked familiar, and I recalled the first time I had been near by to this land; the penny dropped. I realised it was after stepping foot on this land 10 years prior, that the terrifying night visions would begin. The visions of black people covered in blood, injured, and hanging from the trees. I stood reading the sign in shock as it described in detail, word for word what I had seen, night after night for all those years.

I cried painful tears, tears of awe and revelation of what we were really here to do. I cried because I could see the thread joining the dots of my life backwards far beyond any moment that I might have considered a part of this pathway. I cried for the awakening of the internal promise that I now remembered, that I was here to complete the task of sharing my story and the message that comes from the ancestors. I cried because of the pain and suffering of the First Nations people. I cried because it was senseless. I cried because I realised I wasn't crazy, and that this mystical journey was real. The visions I had been seeing for all those years was written for all to see, word for word, what I saw on the sign in front of me. Time folded in half and I could see the past, the present and the future unravelling like threads from a patchwork quilt, all of the pieces of the puzzle of my life, falling into places that I never knew fit.

I was transported back many years to the first time I set foot on the land of the Hawkesbury, the trigger for the beginning of more than a decade of nightmares and visions. At Richmond Hill, I had a realisation of my connection to this place, and the history of what had happened. I now believe that what I had been seeing what happened there. From that day, I never saw the visions again.

Grantlee Kieza, tells us in their book 'Macquarie,' that Macquarie's plan called for men of his 46th Regiment to scale the country from Kurrajong on the north side of the Hawkesbury, to the Five Islands, Illawarra, on the south, and east of the Nepean River. Macquarie's orders were to hit the hostile natives hard around the Nepean, Grose and Hawkesbury Rivers. Captain Schaw was to treat the native people like enemies of war. The orders were that whenever natives were seen, they were to be called upon to surrender themselves as prisoners of war, and *men were to be hung from trees to fill survivors with the greatest of terror.* "The people not content at shooting them in the most treacherous manner in the dark, actually cut a woman's arm off and stripped the scalp on her head over her eyes, and then finding one of the children wounded, deliberately beat the infants brains out with the butt of their musket, the bodies then left in that state, unburied." [1]

Macquarie's ancestors were Scottish, involved in the 1745 Jacobite Rebellion, as were my ancestors, the McDonnell's of Keppoch. Sixteen years before Macquarie's birth, the Jacobite rebellion devastated the Highland clans. The English Government viewed most Highlanders as barbarous and disloyal savages, and the old order of the Highlanders was decimated as the British used the Highland clearances to break up the clan system of self-rule. The British banned traditional Highlander dress, along with the possession of arms and bagpipes, which were deemed to be an instrument of war. Fought on the moorland near Inverness on 16 April 1746, kilted clansman were cut to pieces by the swords, muskets and artillery of the much better equipped and trained English redcoats. The rebellion was over. And now a generation later, a Scotsman, had become the British, inflicting on the native people here, what had been inflicted on his own Highlander ancestors.[2]

What a strange web we weave as humanity, and can we possibly stop?

We begin to see the larger pattern and relationship of perpetrator, perpetrated, played over and over again in history, and our story is no different. Macquarie would tolerate no excuses and ordered three separate military detachments to march into the most remote parts of the colony to punish the hostile natives, by clearing the country of them entirely, and driving them across the mountains, hanging the bodies of those deemed to be criminals.[3] To understand the man Lachlan Macquarie became, is to understand the harsh world in which he grew up, where it was not uncommon for public hangings, drownings, and burnings, all for regular entertainment. Macquarie's biographer, Grantlee Kieza, tells us that in Scotland at the time of Lachlan's birth, memories remained vivid of burned bodies on the roadside, parboiled heads set on spikes. All that happened here in Australia, had happened to the people in Macquarie's own country, to his own Highland people, he now perpetrating atrocities. Throughout history until now, the cycle continues.

It seems that from the days of the Druids, and centuries before, humanity has walked again and again down the path of destruction and desolation. I believe we are at a nexus point in our history, not only within Australia, but in our world as darkness, pain and suffering again reign high. It is time for us to create peace once and for all, for all to sit at the round table of equality, and to return Excalibur to the stone. Let us allow this symbol of hope, of forgiveness, of our deepest humanity and humility to rise again within each and every one of us so that this golden age of peace may begin.

21

STONE OF DESTINY

As I began the completion of this story, I stumbled across some information that connected me to the Queen's coronation, having no knowledge of the wording of this ceremony I was astounded to see that there was a whole section of oaths that included swords. On reading this I felt again compelled to write one last letter, in completion of my task. For months I had thought of writing this letter, though I couldn't seem to find the same inspiration to write in the way I had written the earlier letters.

It wasn't until the morning I learned of the passing of His Royal Highness Prince Philip that I heard the words strongly "you must write now." I got up that morning of the 9th of April and began. It wasn't until I decided to look a little further into the history of one particular sword - the sword of Mercy that the penny dropped - pulling all the threads into one tapestry for me to see how they all connected.

I had decided months ago that much of the following information would go into a second book - though the plan changed when this information came through - the book would not be complete without this letter. The true aim of this whole journey. Just when you think the story is done...Well, you know the rest. And so, this letter below was sent on the 27th of April 2021, and it is hoped that it will stand out amongst the thousands of letters that the Queen is receiving at this time. God speed little letter.

NB: The following information, particularly in relation to Aboriginal places and history served as triggers for my own personal journey, and revelations. I do not wish to collapse their historical meaning, value, or culture into my own belief systems. Merely make note of how they helped me see connectedness to and point to vital truths within my journey.

Miss Jennie Vine
Deputy Correspondence Coordinator
Her Majesty the Queen
Buckingham Palace
London
SW1A, 1AA

Your Majesty,

My name is Angela Sciberras, and this is the latest in a series of letters I have sent since 2018 in regards to my wish to erect a monument of reconciliation at the Wesleyan section of the Wilberforce Cemetery in NSW, and in my quest for an apology from the Crown for the fate that befell Australia's original people as a result of colonisation.

Firstly, may I convey my heartfelt condolences for the loss of your beloved husband Prince Philip. I send warm wishes to you and your family at this extraordinarily sad time. I simply cannot imagine your grief after a lifetime of service together, but I hope your memories will serve to soothe your soul in the difficult days ahead.

I have never connected with my British dreaming. Many of us here in Australia haven't. We continue to tell the tales of the convict, forgetting the legends from which we came and can aspire to. The legends such as King Arthur the once and future king, who led the Knights of the Round Table on a quest to bring peace to the United Kingdoms, and all their people, with a dream to create Albion. I realise now this is my real end – Albion. But only in the sense of the spiritual message and healing its deeper truth can provide.

In his book Arthur Philip: Sailor, Mercenary, Governor, Spy, Michael Pembroke suggests that our first Governor Arthur Philip had a vision for Australia beyond the somewhat double-edged outcome that transpired, which is that of a beautiful country with much to be proud of, but built on the foundations of the tyranny of colonialism, a past yet to be properly told and recognised. Pembroke shares his understanding that Arthur Philip believed in the legend of King Arthur, so much so that he originally wanted Sydney to be named New Albion. Arthur Philip was also a friend of William Wilberforce.

I have come to see how deeply this legend runs in the dreaming of the world. This magical story of King Arthur and the Knights of the Round Table is a part of the fabric of the global myth woven into the tapestry of many countries. I believe we are in the days when Albion needs Arthur most. Or, the world needs Albion more than ever. I thought I knew what Albion was. Though this journey continues to teach me how little I know.

"With the passing of time humanity has entered into a kind of sleep, so much so, that former golden age in which man had enjoyed a magical relationship with the universe has been forgotten, the only evidence of sublime conditions, lying hidden in the myths and legends in which nobody any longer believes."
- Trevor Ravenscroft

Your Majesty, my journey has led me to believe.

Recently, I was guided to purchase a property on 40 acres in the middle of the Yengo National Park, just a couple of hours from Sydney, and only a short drive from a village name St Albans. In fact, the land we now own used to be called St Albans. Upon the establishment of the

British colony at Sydney Cove, this land became Crown Land. It was first purchased and owned by an ex-convict, Aaron Walters, in 1888.

The first time we saw the house, we lifted our eyes after a steep walk uphill and saw a one-of-a-kind stained-glass window. It was filled with all the colours of the rainbow, and all manner of bush animals around the outside of its frame. A frog, possum, butterfly, and snake, woven together with the green leaves of the grape vine, its mauve fruit hanging beneath the canopy. What made the window especially magical was the unicorn at its centre, surrounded by the animals of the Australian bush. One could think this was quite an odd combination, but it was truly breath-taking and like nothing we had ever seen.

A large, handmade mosaic lion stood beneath the stained-glass window, guarding the entry to the house. It reminded me of your Royal Coat of Arms. Without doubt this was a magical place, but did we really want to buy a house two hours away from our hometown of more than 20 years? I turned to my husband and as usual said, "I need a clear sign." Well it didn't take long. We made our way back though the Yengo National Park and decided to stop at one of the roadside produce stalls to purchase refreshments for the long drive home. As we neared civilisation, we slowed at the first sight of a store. We parked directly in front of a massive sign that read Sciberras Fruit and Vegetables.

"Well," my husband laughed. "There's your sign. literally."

Originally the home of the Darkinjung people, once Crown Land, bought by an ex-convict, in the middle of the Yengo National Park. Little did I know how deeply connected this place would be to the path I have been walking, nor that it would ultimately lead me back to you, Your Majesty.

A few days after buying this property, I was working in my Kinesiology clinic with Anna, a friend and colleague who is also a Kinesiologist. Being a Kinesiologist is like working as a detective, joining the dots backwards to a core truth or revelation that can bring healing to a soul. Anna, Scottish by birth and with a beautiful thick accent, was seeking guidance and support in a journey of her own, having been inspired to move to a particular parcel of land at a place named Mount

Keira, though neither of us was prepared for how entwined our stories would be.

The information coming through in the Kinesiology session initially led me to the words Jacob's Ladder. I didn't really know anything about Jacob's Ladder, apart from some vague memories here and there. I did a little research and the sentence connected was receiving the truth hidden in the stone of destiny. I certainly had no idea what the stone of destiny was, nor how it related to Jacob's Ladder, although you might already see the threads of connection. Anna and I were perplexed as to where the session was heading. The information being revealed through the muscle testing process showed a connection to your Coronation, that Jacob's Ladder was associated somehow.

Things started to take shape, as the next piece of information associated was the unicorn. Anna and I contemplated whether this was some symbolic meaning from the unicorn in the stained glass window of our new house, but the next piece of information that followed was the word Iona. I searched for the connection between Iona and the Stone of Destiny and was amazed to find that the Stone of Destiny was said to be kept by the monks of Iona the traditional headquarters of the Scottish Celtic church, until Viking raiders caused them to move to the mainland, first to Dunkeld, Athol, and then to Scone. Here it continued to be used in coronations, as a symbol of Scottish Kingship.[1]

"Angela," Anna whispered to me.

"Do you know what my middle name is?"

"No," I said.

"Iona. My middle name is Iona. I am Anna Iona, and I was conceived on Iona."

Anna and I could start to see this somewhat confusing stream of information forming vital clues of a revelation neither of us was ready to receive. As I scrolled through the research around Iona, and the Stone of Destiny Anna and I continued to connect the dots.

"Okay," we thought to ourselves. "Iona, and the Stone of Destiny are somehow connecting to the legends of Arthur, but how and why?" In gathering information about Iona, a key piece of wording that sprung up was Stirling Castle, its logo a unicorn's head. Again, quite shocked Anna stopped me as soon as this information came forth.

"Angela, my father was heavily involved in the restoration of Stirling Castle, and the re-creation of the famous unicorn tapestries within it."

She explained that some believe the unicorn in the ancient tapestries was a symbol for Christ.[2] In all seriousness your Majesty it seems quite impossible to have such profound, synchronistic connections to this place. It was at this moment in the proceedings that we wondered; what synchronicity had brought the two of us together? Was there some greater depth to the fact that both Anna and I had been guided to move to very special places in our area? I recalled learning that Mount Yengo had been known to Australia's original people as the Uluru of the East, a fascinating fact considering I was only a week away from travelling to Uluru in the Northern Territory to speak of my journey. I mentioned this to Anna and her mouth again opened in shock.

"Angela, do you know how to some Mount Kiera is known to the Aboriginal people around Wollongong?"

"No idea," I said.

"The Uluru of the Illawarra!"

"Oh, my goodness!" I said with wonder.

"What is going on here and why?"

In my search for meaning I found that Mount Yengo was the spiritual centre for the Darkinjung Aboriginal people. It was here that Daramulun was said to have left the earth after creating the Darkinjung land. According to their Dreaming, the land was already there when Daramulun arrived, but it was featureless. He created the land as we see it now with the mountains, rivers, plants and animals. Other flat mountains such as Mt Warong and Mt Warrawalong as well as Burra Gurra (Devil's Rock) are closely associated with Daramulan's visit. He used these mountains as stepping-stones, which is why they are so flat; and he left his footprints on the rocks of Burra Gurra (in the Darkinjung language, Yengo means 'steppingstone' or 'step up').[3]

Burra Gurra (Devil's Rock) is covered with Aboriginal rock engravings including the spirit footprints of Wa-boo-ee (or Baiame), the creator of heaven and earth. In Aboriginal legend he stepped from there to form Mt Yengo in one stride and then ascended back into the sky.[4] We were astounded to think that I was about to travel to Uluru to speak, and had just moved near to a place named the Uluru of the East, and Anna had moved to a place that some called the Uluru of the Illawarra. Even more interesting was the Dreamtime story that Daramulun had used one of those places as a steppingstone back to the sky. To me it felt like a "stairway to heaven?"

I had been booked to speak at a conference on the convergence date 21 December 2020, at least a year before I had come to know the significance of the connection between Arthur, the return of the once and future king, Christ, and this date. This journey to Uluru is a whole other story to be told at another time. I stood in the red soil holding in my hands the forged sword made of the blacksmith – Excalibur returned. I arrived back to my hotel room after a private simple ceremony at Uluru after the great conjunction to see a woman upload a presentation called "The Excalibur Prophecy 21st December 2020." I simply cried. I had travelled all the way to Uluru, been invited to speak about my Journey with Excalibur, stood with this forged sword in the red soil of Uluru under the Great Conjunction Star to come back to my room to once more humbled at the synchronicity. Imagine me laying my head down to rest after all that had occurred to open my phone and immediately see in front of me a notification for the above presentation ending with the following words:

"It is truth that you live by. Truth that you die by, truth that you ascend by. Truth is that which activates the prophesy – for revelations cannot occur without truth. They are intertwined and are one and the same. They are unified, and that is Excalibur. This is the juncture you have come to. Hold the joy of the higher heart, for their lie's truth, and that is Excalibur. Go forward into your solstice star gate point of the 21st December 2020 and fulfil your prophesy."[5]

- Magenta Pixie

This conjunction of Jupiter and Saturn may have an even closer tie to the Biblical story of the birth of Jesus Christ than its occurrence so close to Christmas this year. As noted by Johannes Kepler in the 17th century, a similar conjunction occurred in 7 BCE and could be the astronomical origin of the Star of Bethlehem that guided the wise men. Knowing that Herod the Great had died in 4 BCE, he placed the birth of Christ before that date. And using his knowledge of planetary motion, he found that Jupiter and Saturn underwent a triple conjunction in 7 BCE, that conjunctions of Mars with each planet in 6 BCE were shortly followed by conjunctions of the planets with the sun. Kepler suggests that these solar events aligned with the conjunctions of the planets, and the conception of Christ. That the wise men arrived the following year to witness Christ's birth beneath the Star of Bethlehem.[6] It was here that I began to realise that Albion is, or was not a place to create, but a new level of consciousness awaiting humanity.

My search led me to the connection between Albion and the Cathars. The Cathars were known as Albigensian because of their association with the city of Albi. In 1176 the Church Council declared the Cathar doctrine heretical near Albi. Most of the territory that came to be called Languedoc became attached to the Kingdom of France in the 13th century, following the Albigensian Crusade (1208–1244). The Albigensian crusade sought to end to Vatican considered the Cathar heresy, enabling the Capetian dynasty to extend its influence south. Members of the dynasty were traditionally Catholic, and the early Capetians had an alliance with the Holy Roman Empire, thus the Vatican.[7] Cathars were trapped and burned alive in to eliminate Essene Templar knowledge outside control of the Church.[8]

It has been said that the Cathars were protecting esoteric information in the Gnostic texts and symbols from the Essenes, Christos Templars that accessed hidden energetic templates that allowed a direct connection to communicate with Christos Mission intelligence at that time. As of the Essenes, Christos Templars with the higher purpose to serve and protect the Mother of God principle, the female principle of both Mother Arc and Christos-Sophia, the chalice principle of zero-point flows, a flower grid deep in the planetary grid network and Albion Codes. So, Albion isn't a place?[9]

What esoteric information might we be speaking of? This is where I connect my fathers' symbol, "The Maltese Cross" and the word Albion and I was met with The Albion Code, for the Maltese Cross is also known as the Cathar Cross. The Albion is the androgynous human template created from the twelve spheres of the Tree of Life which, at the fall became buried in the lower dimensional fields of the earth, waiting to be awakened. The Cathar on the other hand is the mother principle of the sound, tone, music, and colours that fill in the Albion spherical architecture. The Cathar is Mother's creation code, the Albion is Father's creation code, and both have to interact and interconnect in Sacred Marriage to birth the Christos-Sophia As they unite in hierogamic union, Mother's sound tones and Holy Spirit can bring colour waves into the base template of the Albion architecture. This sacred union generates new balanced creations throughout the matter worlds, as matter becomes spiritualised through the animating force of the Holy Spirit. Portions of the Cosmic Mother's Universal Body language is called the Cathar. In the Cathar body are multiple star languages containing the instructions set and fire letters for embodiment of the eternal Christos-Sophia template, the time code that is the Universal Mother's creation principle that is inherently coded into the planetary dark matter template, as well as the original human DNA. The blueprint for the world would in its original perfect human body represented in the Human 12 Tree Grid, as the first divine human ever created in a silicate matrix, is called the Albion.[10]

As I sat down to complete this letter, I believed that this is where the revelations ended for now. But in what I thought was the final moments of reviewing my words, a simple search for a reference unlocked a whole new treasure chest of understanding. I discovered a jewel of information that led me to the words I feel called to share with you now. Anna and I were puzzled as to how all of this made any sense when put together. From what we could see, the Stone of Destiny, or what some called the Stone of Scone, had found its place under your very coronation chair. It had, travelled from Scotland after possibly being held at some time in history by the Monks of Iona. But we wondered why. What was it about this stone, and where had its significance come from?

We then learned the Stone of Scone was also known by another name. Jacob's Pillow. According to legend, the sandstone slab was used by the biblical figure Jacob as a pillow when he dreamed of a ladder reaching to heaven. This sandstone was brought to Scotland by way of Egypt, Spain and Ireland. Following his victory at the Battle of Dunbar in 1296, England's King Edward I seized the stone from Scotland's Scone Abbey, and had it fitted into the base of a specially crafted wooden Coronation Chair on which English—and later British—monarchs have been crowned inside London's Westminster Abbey ever since.[11]

The description of Jacob's Ladder appears in Genesis 28: 10-19

"And Jacob went out from Beer Sheeba and went toward Haran. And he lighted upon the place, and tarried there all night, because the sun was set; and he took one of the stones of the place, and put it under his head, and lay down in that place to sleep. And he dreamed, and behold a ladder set up on the earth, and the top of it reached to heaven; and behold the angels of God ascending and descending on it."

— Genesis 28:10–17 Jewish Publication Society (1917)

According to legend, the stone was brought to Scone from Dalriada, (Argyll) by Kenneth Mac Alpin c. 850 A.D. Though it is said that it had previously been brought to Argyll from Ireland by Fergus Mac Erc, a Dalriadan King, sometime in the 5th century. Prior to this it had been transported to Ireland via Spain by Scota, the daughter of an Egyptian Pharaoh; both cautiously identified by Egyptologist Lorraine Evans in her book "Kingdom of the Ark" as Princess Meritaten and her father, Pharaoh Akhenaten. Scota is supposed to have fled Egypt with her Greek husband Gathelos, or Gaidelon, and his followers sometime around 1335 B.C. following a rebellion in which Akhenaten was overthrown by Horemheb, the army commander. The 'Scots,' it is said, after a period in Spain followed by an interval in Ireland, eventually settled in Dalriada and took their name from this Princess Scota, to become the people known throughout history as the 'Scotti.' [12]

Anna and I sat in bewilderment at the story unfolding before us, and the many depictions and theories around this stone and its history. Even as I sit here trying to explain this, I too have moments where I am overwhelmed and lose my understanding. We completed our session, though I spent the coming days continuing to search for more meaning within the puzzle in front of us. Considering I had spent months pondering the idea of Albion and had then been guided to a property that used to be called St Albans I was intrigued. In 303AD, Alban was the first person to be martyred (beheaded by sword) in Britain for preaching Christ's teachings when he substituted himself for Geoffrey of Monmouth, who was spreading Christ's word, contrary to the edict of Roman Emperor Septimius Severus.[13]

I noticed that St. Alban's crest had a sword in it; or a Glave, which was a single-edged blade usually fixed to pole like a spear, which in the 15th century became a way of expressing the word sword. As we know, young Arthur drew Excalibur from The Stone, qualifying him to be King of a then divided land, uniting it for a time with Merlin's help - Merlin representing the Bible and Prophets. "He who draws the Sword from The Stone (of Destiny) shall be King, means quite simply that he who draws the Sword – of the Spirit (God's Truth) from The Stone (Christ – the Rock of Ages) will be King."[14] (Rev 1:16)

So, when Alban was beheaded in place of Geoffrey of Monmouth, for the Word of God, it demonstrated the ultimate self-sacrifice. Symbolically Arthur was the one who extracted the Truth (Sword) from the Words of Christ (The Stone), where the other knights failed, and that qualified him to be King, and to unite the land. It is time now to unite our land. It seems to me there is only one way to reunite the land and that is with truth, love and forgiveness. So why is Christ the Living Stone? Because the Truth, Word, Sword is 'cast in stone,' and is immovable like a rock, like Christ. "Every good gift and every perfect gift are from above, and cometh down from the Father of Light, with whom is no variableness, neither a hint of turning."[15]

All British monarchs since King David were crowned on the Stone of Destiny – The Rock of Ages. Ultimately coronated on the Truth of the Word of God. The key to it all – the truth of the symbolism of the

Sword makes the Roman centurion's spear piercing Jesus' side while on the cross, fit the Sword-in-Stone motif.[16]

I began to realise that Albion was not a place to be created, but a new level of consciousness awaiting humanity. On the 2nd day of June 1953, at the Abbey Church of St. Peter, Westminster you were Coronated and bestowed with sacred swords under oath to God.[17] The Sword of Spiritual Justice, the Sword of the State featuring a crosspiece in the form of a lion and a unicorn, the Sword of Temporal Justice, the Sword of Offerings and the Sword of Mercy.

The Sword of Mercy or Curtana once belonged to Edward the Confessor (1003-1066), one of the last Anglo-Saxon Kings of England before the Norman Conquest of 1066. According to one legend, the Curtana was the sword of Ogier the Dane, an 8th-century warrior. The sword bore the inscription "My name is Cortana, of the same steel and temper as Joyeuse and Durendal." What draws my attention is the legend that links the Sword of Mercy to Tristan, a hero of the Arthurian story, and a Cornish knight of the Round Table. Ogier is said to have inherited Tristan's sword, shortening it and naming it Cortaine. It's also been said that the blade was broken off by an angel to show that a sovereign must show mercy.[18]

"I am Cortana, of the same steel and temper as Joyeuse and Durendal.

The wound is the place where the Light enters you."

— Cassandra Clare

I wondered, what is Joyeuse and Durendal, the answer to which would prove to contain an astounding revelation. The Curtana or sword of Mercy that was bestowed upon you on the day of your coronation, was fabled to contain the steel and temper of the Joyeuse. The Joyeuse was, in medieval legend, the sword wielded by Charlemagne and it had been used in French ceremonies since the thirteenth century. Some legends even claim that the Joyeuse was made with the Lance of Longinus within its Pommel. This was where the unfolding information began to connect. Some may wonder what was or is the Lance of Longinus? Well prepare to be amazed. I searched for information about the Lance to find its other common name – The Holy Lance or Spear of Destiny. The Spear of Destiny was named after Saint Longinus, legendarily known as the lance that pierced the side of Jesus as he hung on the Cross during his Crucifixion. The blade of Joyeuse is said to have been forged from the very same materials as the Durendal, Ogier's Curtana. The name Durendal suggests, along with many other theories, "Dū l-jandal" or "master of the stone." [19] [20]

According to La Chanson de Roland (The Song of Roland), Durendal was brought by an angel to Charlemagne. In that song the sword was said to contain within its golden hilt a tooth of Saint Peter, the blood of St Basil of Caesarea, the hair of Saint Denis and the raiment of Mary, Mother of Jesus.[21] The Children's Book of Warriors told the tale that there was a "priceless thing Charlemagne ever carried in his belt, and that was Joyeuse, the sword which contained in a hilt of gold and gems the head of the lance that pierced our Saviour's Side."[22] On the 2nd day of June 1953, at the Abbey Church of St. Peter, Westminster you were Coronated and bestowed with sacred swords.

"Hear our prayers, O Lord, we beseech thee,
and so direct and support thy servant
Queen ELIZABETH,
that she may not bear the Sword in vain;
but may use it as the minister of God
for the terror and punishment of evildoers,
and for the protection and encouragement of those that do well,
through Jesus Christ our Lord. Amen."

Then shall the Archbishop take the Sword from off the Altar and shall deliver it into the Queen's hands; and, the Queen holding it, the Archbishop shall say:
"Receive this kingly Sword,

brought now from the Altar of God,
and delivered to you by the hands of us
the Bishops and servants of God, though unworthy.
With this sword do justice,
stop the growth of iniquity,
protect the holy Church of God,
help and defend widows and orphans,
restore the things that are gone to decay,
maintain the things that are restored,
punish and reform what is amiss,
and confirm what is in good order:
that doing these things you may be glorious in all virtue;
and so faithfully serve our Lord Jesus Christ in this life,
that you may reign for ever with him
in the life which is to come. Amen." [23]

The symbol of the sword has come as a message in humble relationship to the world at this time and my earlier request in letters gone by. Echoing the words of William Wilberforce, I feel God has set before me Three Great Objects:

1) The completion of: A Sandstone Stone Circle (upon the Wesleyan Section) at Wilberforce Cemetery in NSW, Australia in honour of its namesake, William Wilberforce. A joint creation for the purpose, recognition and reconciliation of the original people of this country.

2) Action of greater significance: To hand this Crown Land, now named The Wesleyan Section where hence forth will stand a memorial and sacred place of remembrance, forgiveness and unity. The days of creating monuments and gardens in the name of peace, with the belief that such a token act be enough to show sincerity, are over.

3) The Miracle: The generation of a full and heartfelt apology from the Crown, for the misdeeds and injustices suffered by First Nations people and settlers of Australia, with the natural and timely ultimate expression of such regret and sincerity, the fulfilment of reconciliation between First Nations the Crown, and all Australian people. In fulfil-

ment of the objectives above, may we victoriously arrive at this monumental outcome whereby we agree it is time for this, a moral and ethical act, an act of good conscience and a demonstration of respect for all humanity, with the overall goal of restoring dignity and sound harmony.

"According to legend associated with the Spear of Destiny, the claimant of this talisman of power has a choice between the service of two opposing spirits in its fulfilment of its world historic aims."

- Trevor Ravenscroft

Whether by fable or truth hidden in plain sight, it is said that he who holds the Spear of Destiny, holds the fate of the world in their hands. A relic of revelation and bridge between the world of sense and the world of spirit.

– Geistliche Welt

Beyond these so-called tales that can be disputed, and mis-proven these items remain as Holy Relics, symbols of your calling and the higher truth that you have promised to uphold. As the most recent Monarch to have been coronated using the Stone of Destiny in 1953 you, Elizabeth II of the United Kingdom of Great Britain and Northern Ireland are called to act upon the Oaths thus taken - Oaths unto God under the symbol of the aforementioned swords. I humbly remind you of your solemn oath to God to: "With this sword do justice, stop the growth of iniquity, help and defend widows and orphans, restore the things that are gone to decay, maintain the things that are restored, punish and reform what is amiss, and confirm what is in good order."

I deeply believe you are destined to become the greatest Queen who ever lived, the Queen who will fulfil one of the greatest prophesies in history by unleashing a flood of forgiveness, redemption, and atonement, bringing long awaited healing to the many. May it be so in God's name. Amen.

Your Faithfully,

Angela Mary Sciberras

The day I posted this letter I noticed that I had received a missed call from a very special friend that I had spent some time with over the prior weekend. While catching up we chatted about a family member who had a near fatal illness and was only due to the family member having heard a male voice say, "call the Ambulance now," that they survived. I liked to think that it was my Dad, but who knows.

So, I realised I had a missed call from my friend just after I had sent the letter. I called her back to see what she was wanting to tell me. Out of the blue she said, "listen I was driving home the other day after our chat, and it came clear as a bell in my mind, "It was your Dad."

We had not talked about my Dad at all in our meeting, but it came to her strongly. She also didn't know of the letter I had just written and sent. She then said, "You know, what just as I had that thought, the strangest thing happening to me while driving. The car in front of me had a **"ladder"** on its roof. Like a work ute. The ladder somehow disconnected from the car, and in front of my eyes got air under it and started to lift up! One end actually slowly lifted to the point it was standing up straight to the sky," she said still reeling from this experience. I sat totally gob smacked to say the least waiting for her to finish her story.

"So, it then flipped off the car in front of me, over my car, and landed between my car and the car behind me! Can you believe that?!" She said...

"Well," I said... "You are not going to believe what I am about to tell you...."

Most will never believe the hundreds of little stories just like that, truly incredible confirmations that all is ok. I'm on track and keep going... I mean who calls you out of the blue to tell you your late father is communicating with us, then simultaneously sees a ladder lift up of the car in front of them, reach up to the sky while doing 70kms an hour - just after I sent a letter to the Queen about Jacobs Ladder. I know... You can't make this... up.

22

MY LETTER TO YOU

"All conflict is rooted in non-acceptance. Accept things as they are, totally and without the slightest judgment. Do not resist anything. In this environment, freedom and wholeness appear, and then whatever must happen will happen. We will know what to do and when to do it. When we have dissolved conflict in complete acceptance, we enter, fully and consciously, the dynamic flowing river of life."

- ROBERT RABBIN

On behalf of my ancestors, who speak through me, who wish to bring peace to all men, and feel the love of forgiveness. On behalf of the whispers of the land that has called me since my birth. This is my divine purpose, and somehow it has led me to you. Help me create the most beautiful story that can be told for a hundred years from now to touch, move and inspire our children's children.

We are entering into a time of profound quickening and transformation. We have come to the edge of what we have known ourselves to be as Australians. We are being beckoned to step into the fire that changes every level of our beings, even the underlying structures of our lives, constitution, and past. Let us step into the unknown and allow this metamorphosis to begin. Allow us at this crossroads to move from the apparent separation between us into reunion. We are in the midst of a personal, national and world revolution, of clearing old patterns, past experiences and judgements, memories and expectations.

It is understood that we may feel at the edge of an invisible wall, as if we are on the crucible of our national and global evolution. There may be times when it seems unbearable. I, like you, might at times want to give up. Be encouraged, as we are truly on the frontier of the unknown. We are truly in the process of transformation and discovering ourselves on new sacred ground. Let us break through all the barriers to union, through all that stands in the way of standing for First Nations people and their sovereignty, for the healing of the past, present and future.

I believe we are on the verge of a great evolutionary jump. Or, you could say we are going through an initiation. After all, isn't an initiation a rite of passage from one level of consciousness to another, and isn't it designed to challenge the very fabric of who we are so we can grow to a greater potential. Maybe when we see, remember and awaken to who we really are, human beings can move as a collective consciousness from a state of surviving to a state of thriving. It is then that we can emerge into our true nature, and fully access our innate capacity as human beings, which is to give, to love, to serve and to take care of one another and the earth.

This story, and wisdom from some of the greatest souls who ever lived, collated together, in no way attempts to seem as if it contains all or any of the answers and evidence of the right way forward, for the one thing that I do know, is that I do not know what is best for Aboriginal people. If we are going to repair a situation, we cannot repair it without doing whatever we can to clean up and heal the past. Time for us to give birth to a brand-new nation and a brand-new world. An inspirational global phenomenon is rising deep from within the human race, we are all feeling it and demonstrating it. We have First Nations people across this land whether you are aware or not, gathering, creating their art, re-learning their language, learning about their land, their mob, and where they come from. It is already happening, with or without us.

John F. Kennedy said "That mankind will end war, or war will end mankind." Can we possibly choose to end this national, global and human war between us to find peace?

My ancestors came here on ships with nothing but the clothes on their backs, and yet look at the thriving nation that has been created from the men and women of those early days. But we must not forget the foundation on which our nation has been built, and we must do whatever it takes to heal and repair the past. We have a special opportunity to journey into the hall of mirrors, to address the parts of ourselves and our history that we have not seen clearly. We have the opportunity to see the unclear, the unacknowledged, the illusion and all of the problems that have come from it. This is our chance to see the truth, complete unfinished business and listen. It is time for us to truly look into the mirror that reveals all that has been left so that we may see the shadow parts of ourselves and the nation's history so that we may be able to stand in the light of truth. We are now being given the privilege and gift of insight.

Your Sister,
Angela Mary Sciberras (Shrimpton)
Kin 22: White Solar Wind
Born: Cosmic Moon 28
Blue Planetary Storm Year
I pulse in order to communicate
Realising breath
I seal the input of Spirit
With the Solar Tone of Intention
I am guided by Endlessness
I am a Galactic Activation Portal Enter Me

23

NOW THEY SEND YOU FORTH

"We are the heroes of our time, but we're dancing with the demons in our minds."

- MÅNS ZELMERLÖW

To all those who have ears to hear, and eyes to see. You have journeyed with me through time and space, synchronicity and happenstance, and it is my deep hope that you will now, having walked this path, feel within you the call. The call to stand together; united as the rainbow nation of all colours and people of our world, unique in our expressions.

I completed the first draft of this book minus one chapter, this one, this letter to you. You see I didn't know what it was to be yet, I wasn't yet clear how I could possibly express all that I see within myself and imagine what God was showing me. I sent the other chapters off for the editing process to begin, though I hadn't even begun to write this final chapter, possibly the most important in the entire journey for one main reason, I had one piece of the puzzle remaining, you. We are step-ping into the dreaming, the dreaming that we are all dreaming together, that is dreaming us. It was perfect, and so I went to bed exhausted but at peace.

As we come to what may seem like the end of this story, I wonder, what am I to say to the people of Australia? To the descendants of the tribes of the fleets who settled this land. What am I to say to the tribes and nations of the world? A vision entered my mind. A single White Stag stood staring at me, the purity, and the energy beyond anything I can express or explain. Stag was in the painting, we learned about White Stag, but how would this become the energy foundation of the words I would now say to you? What is it that White Stag requests of us?

White Stag is not a story nor legend, but a spiritual truth that has been passed from generation to generation. In all parts of the world there are legends filled with metaphors, symbols and mythologies that correlate across all cultures, this much more than synchronicity. These are pieces of one puzzle, connecting us under one sky upon the earth. So too, this legend of the sacredness of White Stag crossing the hands of time and space with the most important message of our age, a mes-sage for us to decipher and answer.

Associated with the sun, and in early Christian icons the sun ap-pears between its antlers. In Celtic mythology, the stag is a magical creature that can move between the worlds, many tales having been told of humans transforming into deer. The Welsh tell the tale of Culh-wch and Olwen, the stag being one of the oldest animals in the world, along with the blackbird, owl, eagle and salmon. The antlers on the White Stag are compared to tree-branches and thus may represent fer-tility, since they are shed and re-grown year after year.[1]

In Native teachings White Stag is sacred, therefore, to be respected and not killed or else the hunter can easily be the hunted. A King's en-counter with a mystical White Stag in an Edinburgh forest 900 years ago has left a rich legend and legacy that still endures. Depictions of the creature can still be seen dotted around the city. They mark the incident said to have taken place on Holy Cross Day, September 14, 1128, in the ancient forest of Drumsheugh which then covered vast swathes of land around Salisbury Crags. In Arthurian legend, the White Stag is an animal that can never be caught and represents the quest for spiritual knowledge. White Stag is a spiritual truth that has been passed down from generation to generation by the people. [1]

The Native Americans believed the occurrence of a white animal was a huge sign of prophecy from the Great Spirit that a major shift in the world had come. Usually, white animals were seen during soul or vision quests. However, if one was to be seen during the normal course of the day, this would cause a tremendous ripple among the tribe. A meeting would be called, the elders would be consulted, and great care would be taken to communicate with the animal spirits and old people to determine the meaning of the message. [2]

On the same day I received this vision, I ventured out for a break. I sat down to enjoy a coffee and some down time, flipping through the pages of the newspaper resting on the bench. There, plain as day within the Telegraph was an article about a White Joey named Angel, rescued by the Little Urchins Wildlife Sanctuary in Reedy Creek, North Melbourne. I sat and smiled at the little picture of the pure white kangaroo. I mean what are the chances. And so, I had my confirmation that the message I was receiving was to be trusted and acted upon, thanks to a little white kangaroo.

This is why I believe that the White Stag has come to me now and wishes to come to you. It symbolises the time to come together to consult, to gather with the elders of this land, to listen, learn and to take care to communicate with each other. It is time to listen, learn and act from unconditional radical love. It is time to come together and gather as one people of the rainbow nations of the world. It is time to make peace, and truly listen to the voice of our mother as she cries.

I call upon the rainbow nations of Australia, in particular, the descendants of the tribes of the nations of people who came here from every direction of the globe. Those tribes that came on ships from afar from 1788 onwards. Do you hear the voice of your ancestors calling you?

Then rise up in their name, on their behalf with love and humility. Each ship that arrived on these shores, carrying people from lands of the legends I have shared with you in these pages. These words and stories have been shared to awaken your ancient souls, to reconnect us to our old people, to hear their voices and choose to take loving action to make things right. It is time to break the cycle of pain and suffering and heal the land and each other.

Some may consider the notion of creating a stone circle of healing and remembrance to be a continuance of settler's ways of doing things. But this was never the reason for me to share this vision. I share it because it is the story within my bones, with the ability to awaken me to my greatest potential. It is only one's ignorance that would have us think that we of Europe were the only people to create sacred stone circles, and indeed there were examples of stone circles found here when our ancestors arrived in Australia. Indeed, stone arrangements were found across the country.

As my respected Elder and mentor, Uncle Greg Simms taught me:

"Aboriginal people are the greatest counsellors and psychologists the world has ever known, greatest conservationists, world's greatest scientists and astronomers, that's the Aboriginal people. As we take our next step, let us remember the ones that walked this sacred land before. We have over 500 dialects in this country, in NSW we have over 136, so this must have been a multicultural country before settlers came here in 1788 and the ones that followed. And in saying this we are all Australians, and we as Aboriginal Elders, don't exclude people from the circle. We love people to come and share their values and stories. We learn from our old people, from our stories, songs and dance that belong to all people, not just the Aboriginal people. We will never have knowledge if we don't do this. Once we start learning from each other, then we are heading in the right direction towards reconciliation. And don't you think the music would sound much better if we use both the black and white keys?"

And so, in remembrance of those ancient ones who walked this sacred land before us, for tens of thousands of years. Those ancient ones who still walk among us. I call upon our ancestors of the tribes of the fleets to come forth. From the First Fleet that arrived in January 1788.

The descendants of the souls of the Alexander, Borrowdale, Charlotte, Fishburn, Friendship, Golden Grove, HMS Sirius, HMS Supply, Lady Penrhyn, Prince of Wales, Scarborough and its 1420 souls we call on you now.

Calling upon the descendants of the tribes of the six ships of the Second Fleet which arrived in Australia in June 1790, Lady Juliana, Guardian, Justinian, Suprize, Neptune and Scarborough. Of the 1006 convict souls who arrived here in 1790, 40 percent were dead within the first 6 months.

Calling upon the descendants of the tribes of the 11 ships of the Third Fleet which arrived in Australia in 1791, Atlantic, William and Ann, Britannia, Matilda, Salamander, Albemarle, Mary Anne, Admiral Barrington, Active, Queen and HMS Gorgon carrying over 2,000 souls. There are many more arrivals over the years of settlement, and it would be almost impossible to mention them all. Some include the first shipload of Irish convicts, which left for New South Wales in April 1791. Between 1791 and 1853 approximately 26,500 Irish people were transported to New South Wales, many for trivial offences. The ships and settlers that have come from across the world, as convicts, free settlers and explorers, I call upon you now, the descendants of these people, I call upon each and every one of you who find that these symbols and messages touch your heart. I call upon all those who have ancestors who have arrived here, in whatever way they came, in whatever way they became a part of this rainbow nation of tribes and people from across the globe. I call upon you.

I see now that it is not through the dream of one woman, but the dreaming of millions of souls or more that we can create this miracle. One voice, my voice, was not enough to move the mountain. I am just one person, one voice, but now I see that together, descendants of the fleets and all those who came here from England, Wales, Ireland, Scotland and so many other nations, so many others who wish to be heard, to make the past right we can stand together united for peace.

And I wonder what if there were more voices. Voices of all kinds, sounds and perspectives. What if there were millions of voices of the ancestors. What if there was your voice, inspired to take your Excalibur of truth, love, bravery and honour. What if you placed it in your backbone and stood together. Grails filled and overflowing with good will, love and generosity, the sacred chalice, open and ready to receive all of the blessings that come with letting go, facing your fears and becoming unconditional love in the face of non-agreement. Arthur is a consciousness, and Albion is the place of peace we can create in our hearts and world. Let the once and future King rise again within us all, it is time.

If you are moved and inspired I will, at the end of this book show you where you can send your letters. Imagine a letter from the descendants of each and every soul, convict, sailor and official who arrived here on the ships, or whatever way your people came. Their voices heard, your voices heard. Imagine being generation to do what it takes, no matter what it costs to make things right, and in the doing, so letting grace fall upon us. Imagine beautiful leather bound books, filled with thousands of letters, presented to the Prime Minister and Governor General of Australia, and, the Queen of England. Thank you for journeying with me through this work, the greatest work. The most honoured privilege to heal our family lines, not only for our future, but for our ancestors as well. I applaud you; I celebrate you. It is my belief that this journey that started with a package arriving on my father's doorstep in 1998 has been for a far greater purpose than I could have ever imagined, and the journey has barely begun. It is my belief that it is only now that the story shall truly reveal itself, through you, through us all.

Whenever I feel afraid of the days ahead, I take comfort from the words and bravery of Robert Kennedy, in particular the courage shown on April 4, 1968, the day Martin Luther King was shot and killed. On that night, New York senator Robert F. Kennedy wanted to deliver the news to the people of Indianapolis. The local police warned they would not be able to protect him if a riot broke out, as he was in the heart of an African American ghetto. Writing notes on the ride there, he started the speech without any drafts or prewritten words. This speech was delivered on the back of a flatbed truck, and although many major cities rioted, Indianapolis remained calm after RFK's speech. Just 63 days later, he was assassinated. When I first heard his words I had the most profound energy come over me. As tears fell down my face, I saw in my imagination Robert at my side, immaculate in a black suit and Dr King beside him. I imagined he might say:

"These words were timely then, and may they be timely now. For in truth they are timeless. We are with you all."

Robert sought peace. He sought to stand for all that Dr King lived for, and that which they both died. Peace. Kennedy said: *"In this difficult time for the world, it's perhaps well to ask what kind of a nation, what kind of world we are and what direction you want to move in. For those of you who are black, considering the evidence is that white people were responsible for the atrocities of the past, one could be filled with bitterness, hatred, and a desire for revenge. You can move in that direction as a country if you wish, towards even greater polarisation, black people against whites, and white people against blacks, filled with hatred toward one another. Or you can choose to make an effort, just as Martin Luther King did, to seek to understand, comprehend, and replace violence, that stain of bloodshed that has spread across our land, with understanding, compassion and love."*

Kennedy's favourite poet, Aeschylus once wrote, *"Even in our sleep, pain which we cannot forget, falls drop by drop upon the heart, until, in our own despair, against our will, comes wisdom through the awful grace of God."* [3]

"Garlugun Girrwaa Yuludarla — Onemobdreaming, is the dreaming of all people uniting together upon country in proper way, living by the universal laws passed down by our ancestors of how to live on the mother together in harmony. They may be old ways, but we can work together. To bring unity back into the world community."
- Uncle Allan Phillips
Imagine a million dreams, a million dreamers, imagine a million let-

ters. We could send a ripple of love through our country and make history. It is time for Australia, like the Phoenix, to rise! The journey has just begun, let's see what we can create together, as One Mob!

Your sister in Light,

Angela Sciberras (Shrimpton)
Letter completed: 30 December 2019
Kin 172: Yellow Electric Human
I activate in order to influence
Bonding wisdom
I seal the process of free will
With the electric tone of service
I am guided by the power of intelligence.

In Memory of

WILLIAM WILBERFORCE

BORN IN HULL AUGUST 24TH 1759
DIED IN LONDON JULY 29TH 1833

"The tiny trickle from Wilberforce's ducts had loosed a diluvian apocalypse never before seen in the chamber. But it was an apocalypse not of judgement, but of grace. It was as if the entire nation, as if the entire empire that circled the human globe was in flood of tears and huzzahs. Baptised, sanctified and marked forever for what they were now doing."

- ERIC METAXAS

BEGIN THE STORY

"The work of the eyes is done. Go now and do the heart-work on the images imprisoned within you."

- RAINER MARIA RILKE

For those inspired with their own words / letter and wonder where you could send it:

(Her Majesty the Queen)
C/O ANGELA SCIBERRAS
PO BOX 154
KINGSWOOD
NSW 2747
AUSTRALIA

Like the days of old, there is something to putting pen to paper, or typing, printing and signing a letter, sent by hand, delivered by hand having made a journey. We would prefer physical letters, though if you for some reason cannot do so, you can email your letter to: info@newrealmz.com. Letters sent with loving intention will be bound in series of books to be released at some time in the future with the intention to flood our world and nation with love and healing from one another. They will also come together to be handed to our Governor General and the Queen. If these compilations are published, all profits will go towards supporting the outreach such as the Onemobdreaming Foundation. Its programs advance human and environmental health, and well being through education. Please provide contact details so that I can remain in communication with you, though your personal information will not be shared without expressed permission. I thank you. Imagine a million dreamers, a million dreams, a million letters to the Queen.

If you would like more information about the Onemobdreaming Foundation (Garlugun Girrwaa Yuludarla) please contact its Founder Uncle Allan Phillips at www.onemobdreaming.com

"Together we will - Onemobdreaming"
- Allan James Phillips

GRATITUDE

"I am circling around God, around the ancient tower, and I have been cir-
cling for a thousand years, and I still don't know if I am a falcon, or a storm,
or a great song."

— RAINER MARIA RILKE

To my Mother Irene, there are simply no words to describe the deep love and profound gratitude I have for you. You are my best friend, and unwavering support of all and any of the so-called hair brained ideas and things I get up to. Thank you for always loving me unconditionally. For being proud of me as a daughter and believing in me as a soul with a purpose here on earth. Thank you for giving me the gift of life, and always being just as excited about my projects as I am; no matter how crazy. I will never be able to show the depths of my love and gratitude to my Stepfather Trevor and yourself for your support.

I thank Lindy and Mervyn Clifton and family, for their undying, and boundless love of me and my path. I could never have achieved the jewels of my life without you both. I love and thank you with all my heart. In extension I thank Lindy's parents the late Don and Mary Davis, who's dedication to their spiritual path, to serving others and our world has been key in all that I do to love and support others. "Two hearts working as one, to assist, serve and enlighten all who crossed their pathways, your love and legacy lives on in countless others."

To my sisters Erika and Niesha, thank you for your love and support, particularly during the difficult time of the loss of our father. I love you both. Thank you Niesha for all the hard work you have done over the years on the family tree, exploring and discovering the roots and history of our descendants, I could never have pulled all this together without you, thank you.

To one of my most cherished friends Renee. You have been my backbone and safe place to fall for many years now and I know I could never have kept standing for my journey and myself without your unconditional love, and fierce support. This deep thanks extends with all my heart to my cherished friend Nikkola, (and Michael) your fiery love and support of me has me able to be who I am today. I dedicate this work to you with all my heart and gratitude.

Joanne, Rosemary, and Susan. I have no idea how to express the well of love that exists for you three. From the moment we found each other again in this lifetime you have been my constant companions, and loving stand for me as a soul and human being. Without your love, your joy, your compassion, your dedication and unwavering friendship I simply cannot imagine what life would have been like. I would not have survived it that is what I know for sure. I will never be able to thank you enough and dedicate this work to you also as an extension of our life's work together. Thank you also to the community of Dreamweaver's who have held this vision. To each and every one I send love. To my bud Kelly, you have been a loyal and compassionate friend who has always seen the good in me no matter what. I'll never be able to thank you and Linda enough for always believing and standing for the journey we have all been on, no matter how hard it sometimes became. I dedicate this to you.

To my late father Colin Anthony Shrimpton. I stood at your grave in Eugowra just the other day and wondered, how did you end up in there so soon. I still cannot believe it. And I miss you every single moment of every day. No matter how crazy my life sometimes seemed, when I felt afraid to be myself, you always said the same thing. "Ange, back yourself."

I cannot tell you how many times in this journey I was about to give up and give in, when I would hear your voice in my mind. "Ange, back yourself." And I would. I may not win, this book may or may not be a runaway success and New York Times Best Seller. But I did it, I did what I said I would do. And no matter how scared I was, or how afraid I was to fail. I backed myself. And so ultimately, I win in the end. I win myself. Because as you always taught me, to press on, your favourite quote by Calvin Coolidge;

"Nothing in the world can take the place of persistence. Talent will not, nothing is more common than unsuccessful men with talent. Genius will not, unrewarded genius is almost a proverb. Education will not, the world is full of educated derelicts. Persistence and determination alone are omnipotent."

I dedicate this work to you and all our ancestor's. I so wish you were here to see where all this has ended up, even though there is still so far to go on the journey before I will see you once more and join you all in spirit. As much as I look forward to that reunion, I will keep working until my time is done here, and our great commission complete. Thank you for all you have given me, I love you and dedicate this to you.

To my husband Steve without whom I would not have had the support to dedicate the time and space over many years to develop my gifts and talents, to spent countless unpaid hours in hospitals and at bedsides with dying people. To complete this work, hundreds of hours writing. Without your love and support I know that I would never have been able to complete this task. I am profoundly grateful to you and will never be able to thank you enough for all you have done for me, which has freed me to help so many other people. I love and thank you and the family with all my heart. I dedicate this work and its outcomes to you. Feel proud and accomplished, and know you played a vital role in its manifestation. I hope as it unfolds you will finally see the method in my madness, and the love in every action along the way. Thank you deeply.

Kathryn and Mick. Through the gift of playing sacred harp at Uluru I was divinely led Uluru to meet Uncle Allan, a powerful and critical ally in this journey. Kathryn you will never know how pivotal it was, to share this story with you, while it still lived in my head only, and before I had written in down on paper. At the completion of the short version of a very long tale you said..."Angela, that is the greatest story, never told." I fought it for a while, but in the end, your famous words rang true for me, many are welcome to disagree, that's ok, though as you now see, your words grace the title page. Thank you. Your unwavering belief in me and the story will forever be cherished.

Deep thanks must go to my mentor and Uncle, Aboriginal Elder Greg Simms. It has been your unconditional love, support and belief in me that has brought a miracle from my bones. I dedicate this book and its outcome to you, and the countless First Nations people past, present and future. These words and actions come from the deepest place in the wellspring of my heart, and I am boundlessly grateful that no matter what, no matter my fears, you always smiled at me and called me deadly. I also thank all the other Aunties and Uncles that have taught me so much over the last few years.

To Uncle Allan and Onemobdreaming, there are simply no words to describe how grateful and humbled I am to have such a great friend, mentor and teacher as you. Thank you from the bottom of my heart for always having time to hear my raving and ranting while walking this sometimes confusing, frightening and difficult road. Your sage words always put me back on the right path and kept me on the red road to complete this task. I will never be able to thank you enough for attending my father's funeral, and for connecting me to Worimii Elder Uncle Richard. The love, and support has been a divine gift. I dedicate this work to you, and the blossoming of your vision Onemobdreaming.

To Francine, and Blue Ray Soul Paintings. The timing and prophetic nature of your art will be forever cherished as one of the most important keys to doorways along the road of this journey. Your gifts and artistic talent bless so many, and I am profoundly grateful that you gifted me with my painting at a vital moment in this story. I thank you and honour your gift. I dedicate this work to you and the world of spirit that speak through you.

Deep thanks go to our Blacksmith Geoff from Zenptah Swords for co-creating Excalibur with such devotion and care. Thank you for believing, and being such a magical part of this journey, I am profoundly honoured and grateful to connect to a fellow descendant of an ancestor who braved the ocean to arrive here on the Scarborough all those years ago. May we do them proud.

To my endless list of friends, family members, and supporters I thank you with all my heart, in particular my dear friend Elizabeth. For without our journey, this miraculous tale would never have been told. I dedicate this to you, and Terry with love. You have taught me the greatest lesson of my life, love never fails and can overcome time, space and even death.

There have been times when I have feared I was losing my mind or wondered if people might think I am crazy with all of this. And they are entitled to their thoughts and opinions. In those painful moments I was often led back to the words of my mentor the late Robert Rabbin, who shared this pearl one evening while on a coaching call from the USA. After I expressed my fear being out of my mind, Robert rolled his eyes, sighed and said "Angela the expression, out of your mind is misused. The crazy train is not full of people "out of their mind" but of people in their mind. There are only a few people per million who are truly out of the mind, that is a blessed state. May it happen to you." And so, Robert, I let go, and have experienced the bliss that is the cosmic roar, the cosmic cornucopia and cauldron of crazy. Thank you, my dear friend. I just know your helping me from the other side of the veil, regularly kicking my butt. Without your love, support, and fierce belief in me, I am quite sure I would never have found the fire within myself, never found the shakti you so loved to release in others, never been so bold, so courageous to have completed this task.

"Drink Deeply" you would say, "if you are intoxicated enough, the words will flow Angela. If you're exceptionally drunk, what will come forth will be exquisite. Quench your thirst from this well Angela" There are few in the world who will believe in us enough, love us enough to ask us to do the hard things, help us face our greatest fears, and become everything, say everything and leave this world an empty vessel. Our soul poured out amongst those left in the world.

Now Robert, along with all the ancestors, you are living in the shimmering light of your true self. The truth of the matter was YOU were a SACRED HUB. You were that untapped, untamed, unleashed soul who with his mere presence unleashed those around him into the love of their own voice, their message, but more than that, the truth that there is no message, you are the message. If what they say is true, that we are the sum total of the people we love and our experiences in life, I'm so honoured to have you all, each and every one of you be a part of me. And I'll keep doing my best to do as Robert asked me. I hope that this book shows that I listened, learned and now pass on your teaching's to: Be Present, Pay Attention, Listen Deeply, Speak Truthfully and Act Creatively.

I also wish to thank my cherished friend Anikiko for adding what I have always known from the moment I first met you was "the voice that could heal the world," to our little promotional video. Thank you for being such a powerful support in my transformation and growth in this life. You are simply, the Queen of Frequency. Thank you for adding yours to this creation, with all my love.

I thank Karen and Jack for believing in me so much you thought I should make a little movie... And we did! Love you both so much for bringing Tim an the crew into this wonderful journey to help us make magic on film. I am so grateful I am so proud of what we all created together. Thank you Emma Nally, my website, and book cover designer. Your patience and unwavering support has been so moving. Thank you so very much with all my heart. I also thank Anna Iona... The final key, to the final revelation. I bow in deep gratitude.

Thank you Jodie Simpson for the final touch of our codes... I know they filled the air and the journey with so much beautiful magic.

How could I not succeed with souls standing for me like that? And it is for you, and the many others who have loved, encouraged and supported me that I do this. And so, it is here that I end this dedication to those who played the most important, yet unseen and unheard part of this story. To all those unseen and unheard, I see you and I hear you and I now pass on your message, as instructed to all those with ears to hear and eyes to see.

This story has but scratched the surface of the pain, absolute chaos and colossal suffering that your ancient society was plunged into in 1788. Because of you, the ones that survived, the sacred fire continues to burn, and it is my deep hope that because of you, your future generations and all of Australia will thrive. We honour you, your ancestors and elder's past, present and emerging. My I be so humble to hope, that I may, as Eric Metaxas says of William Wilberforce at his realisation of the Abolishment of the Slave Trade "Be a wo[man] allowed the rarest privilege to be awake in side my own dream" [1]

"I have a humble dream to have earned the right to lay my bones within the mother, along with all my ancestors of the fleets in peace knowing we have done our small part to mend and heal one another. And so, we complete this transmission of thanksgiving with boundless, unconditional love, may I be so honoured to have achieved this one and only task. Amen."
- Angela Sciberras

Angela Mary Sciberras (Shrimpton)
White Solar Wind - Messenger of the Ancestors of the Tribes of the Boats of Avalon

First Transmission Complete 31st December 2019 at 5.33pm
Rhythmic Moon 19
Year of The White Magnetic Wizard - Kin 172: Yellow Electric Human
- I activate in order to influence
Bonding wisdom
I seal the process of free will
With the electric tone of service
I am guided by the power of intelligence.

Last Transmission and Edit Completed 29th April 2021
Planetary Moon 26
Year of the Blue Planetary Storm - Kin 136: Yellow Rhythmic Warrior
I organise in order to question

Balancing fearlessness
I seal the output of intelligence
With the rhythmic tone of equality

Whole and complete
Spectral Moon 4
Year of the Blue Lunar Storm - Kin 142 White Crystal Wind
I dedicate in order to communicate
Universalising breath
I seal the input of Spirit
With the crystal tone of cooperation
I am guided by timelessness.

Tag your it....

NOTES

CHAPTER 7

1) Browning, Yvonne, Anne Williams, and Clarence Pittard. 1990. *St. Peters Richmond: the early people and burials 1791-1855*. [Mullion Creek, N.S.W.]: Y. Browning. p12-13

CHAPTER 9

1) Simms, Greg. Uncle Greg Simms. 2017, University of Western Sydney Webpage.
https://www.westernsydney.edu.au/oatsiee/aboriginal_and_torres_strait_islander_employment_and_engagement/gok_profiles/a_-_z_listing/uncle_greg_simms

CHAPTER 10

1) Eric Metaxas. *Amazing Grace. William Wilberforce and the Heroic Campaign to End Slavery*. Harper Collins Publishers, 2007. Introduction.

2) BBC - "Historic Figures William Wilberforce," Historical, BBC HISTORY, n.d., (http://www.bbc.co.uk/history/historic_figures/wilberforce_william.shtml).

3) Eric Metaxas. *Amazing Grace. William Wilberforce and the Heroic Campaign to End Slavery*. Harper Collins Publishers, 2007. 277

4) Eric Metaxas. *Amazing Grace. William Wilberforce and the Heroic Campaign to End Slavery*. Harper Collins Publishers, 2007. p144

5) Eric Metaxas. *Amazing Grace. William Wilberforce and the Heroic Campaign to End Slavery*. Harper Collins Publishers, 2007. p144

6) Belmont, Kevin. 2002. Why William Wilberforce was a Hero for Humanity. YouTube presentation. https://youtu.be/ofDJheWgboI

7) Belmont, Kevin. 2002. Why William Wilberforce was a Hero for Humanity. You tube presentation. https://youtu.be/ofDJheWgboI

CHAPTER 11

1) Bruce Elder.1988. *Blood on the Wattle. Massacres and Maltreatment of Australian*

Aborigines since 1788. (The Myall Creek Massacre) Child & Associates Publishing. Aust. Pg. 73

2) Bruce Elder.1988. *Blood on the Wattle. Massacres and Maltreatment of Australian Aborigines since 1788. (The Myall Creek Massacre)* Child & Associates Publishing. Pg. 80

3) Bruce Elder.1988. *Blood on the Wattle. Massacres and Maltreatment of Australian Aborigines since 1788. (The Myall Creek Massacre)* Child & Associates Publishing. Pg. 82

4) Bruce Elder.1988. *Blood on the Wattle. Massacres and Maltreatment of Australian Aborigines since 1788. (The Myall Creek Massacre)* Child & Associates Publishing. Pg. 82

CHAPTER 12

1) Scott Alexander King. *Animal Messengers: Interpreting the Symbolic Language of the Worlds Animals.* New Holland Publishers, 2016. p336

2) Phillips, Allan, 2019. One Mob Dreaming. https://www.onemobdreaming.com/index.html. Recorded phone conversation, January 2020.

CHAPTER 16

1) http://www.ambulance.nsw.gov.au/about-us/History/History-of-the-Maltese-Cross.html

2) Mythologian.net. Maltese Cross Symbol, Its Meaning, History and Relation to The Firefighter Emblem. https://mythologian.net/maltese-cross-symbol-meaning-history-maltese-cross-sign-firefighter-emblem/

3) Mythologian.net. Maltese Cross Symbol, Its Meaning, History and Relation to The Firefighter Emblem. https://mythologian.net/maltese-cross-symbol-meaning-history-maltese-cross-sign-firefighter-emblem/

4) John Paul II. 2000. Homily on the Day of Pardon in the Holy Year 2000 (12th March).

CHAPTER 17

1) Susan Morgan Black. "The Order of Bards, Ovates and Druids," December 19, 2019. https://www.druidry.org/library/gods-goddesses/brigit.

2) Scott Alexander King. *Animal Messengers: Interpreting the Symbolic Language of the Worlds Animals.* New Holland Publishers, 2016. p334

3) Magenta Pixie. "Queen Sophia, Princess Aurora, the Merlin Excalibur Codex. Krystal Stargate Series Part 5)." You Tube. *The Merlin Excalibur Codex* (blog), November 25, 2019. https://youtu.be/p2UAKTGMJ10.

CHAPTER 18

1) Scribed by Helen Schucman, *A Course in Miracles* (New York: Viking: The Foundation for Inner Peace: Foundation for Inner Peace, 1976).

2) David John Randall, "Edward Field - Marine Scarborough 1970." Historical Geni, May 24, 2018, https://www.geni.com/people/Edward-Field-Marine-Scarborough-1790/

3) David John Randall, "Edward Field." ibid

4) https://www.smh.com.au/entertainment/books/the-secrets-and-dreams-of-our-first-governor-20131003-2uvlv.html) Caterson, Simon. 2013. The Secrets and Dreams of our First Governor. Sydney Morning Herald.

CHAPTER 19

1) Pembroke, Michael. 2013. Arthur Phillip: Sailor, Mercenary, Governor, Spy. Hardie Grant Books. p 1

2) Pembroke, Michael. 2013. Arthur Phillip: Sailor, Mercenary, Governor, Spy. Hardie Grant Books. p ix

3) Pembroke, Michael. 2013. Arthur Phillip: Sailor, Mercenary, Governor, Spy. Hardie Grant Books. p 148

4) Pembroke, Michael. 2013. Arthur Phillip: Sailor, Mercenary, Governor, Spy. Hardie Grant Books. p 206

CHAPTER 20

1) Monument Hill, 2020. Battle of Richmond Hill. https://monumentaustralia.org.au/themes/conflict/Indigenous/display/93434-battle-of-richmond-hill)

2) Kieza, Grantlee. 2019. Macquarie: lover, fighter, nation builder, autocrat. ABC Books. p 387

3) Kieza, Grantlee. 2019. Macquarie: lover, fighter, nation builder, autocrat. ABC Books. p 386

CHAPTER 21

1) Wikipedia contributors, "Westminster Stone theory," Wikipedia, The Free Encyclopedia, https://en.wikipedia.org/w/index.php?title=Westminster_Stone_theory&oldid=997002131 (accessed May 2, 2021).

2) Beal, Jane. 2019. Analysis of "The Lady and the Unicorn" Tapestries from "The Unicorn as a Symbol for Christ in Medieval Culture." www.janebeal.wordpress.com

3) http://visitsydneyaustralia.com.au/wollombi.html

4) http://visitsydneyaustralia.com.au/wollombi.html

5) Magenta Pixie: Excalibur Stargate Activations 21st December 2020. https://youtu.be/NYmgPHaaAQo

6) Daryl, Janzen. 2020 'The Christmas Star Appears Again. Jupiter and Saturn Align I the Great Conjunction Dec 21st, 2020.' The Conversation Online Edition. https://theconversation.com/the-christmas-star-appears-again-jupiter-and-saturn-align-in-the-great-conjunction-on-dec-21-2020-152370 (accessed December 23rd, 2020)

7) http://www.thesonsofscotland.co.uk/thestoneofdestiny.htm

8) https://energeticsynthesis.com/index.php/resource-tools/blog-timeline-shift/3433-cathars-in-france

9) https://energeticsynthesis.com/index.php/resource-tools/blog-timeline-shift/ 3433-cathars-in-france

10) https://energeticsynthesis.com/index.php/resource-tools/blog-timeline-shift/ 3433-cathars-in-france

11)Wikipedia contributors, "Westminster Stone theory," *Wikipedia, The Free Encyclopedia*, https://en.wikipedia.org/w/index.php?title=Westminster_Stone_theory&oldid=997002131 (accessed May 2, 2021).

12) https://www.ancientpages.com/2017/07/16/curtana-sword-mercy-belonged-anglo-saxon-king-edward-confessor-perhaps-even-arthurian-hero-tristan/

13) Bullfinch's Mythology, Legends of Charlemagne, Chapter 24

Wikipedia contributors, "Saint Alban," *Wikipedia, The Free Encyclopedia*, https://en.wikipedia.org/w/index.php?title=Saint_Alban&oldid=1015837184

(accessed May 2, 2021).

14) Philip. August 5, 2015. 'What's in the Crest. Excalibur & the Stone of Destiny at St Alban's' Analysis from a St. Albans College ex Pupil. https://stalbanscollegesymbols.wordpress.com/2015/08/05/meanings-behind-the-symbols/ (accessed April 20, 2020)

15) Philip. August 5, 2015. 'What's in the Crest. Excalibur & the Stone of Destiny at St Alban's' Analysis from a St. Albans College ex Pupil. https://stalbanscollegesymbols.wordpress.com/2015/08/05/meanings-behind-the-symbols/ (accessed April 20, 2020)

16) Philip. August 5, 2015. 'What's in the Crest. Excalibur & the Stone of Destiny at St Alban's' Analysis from a St. Albans College ex Pupil. https://stalbanscollegesymbols.wordpress.com/2015/08/05/meanings-behind-the-symbols/ (accessed April 20, 2020)

17) Oremus: Anglican Liturgical Library. *The Form and Order of Service that is to be performed and the Ceremonies that are to be observed in The Coronation of Her Majesty Queen Elizabeth II in the Abbey Church of St. Peter, Westminster, on Tuesday, the second day of June 1953. http://www.oremus.org/liturgy/coronation/cor1953b.html (accessed March 2021)*

18) Charlotte. November 18, 2015. Just History 'Curtana.' http://www.history-naked.com/curtana/ (accessed April 2021)

19) Bellamy, James A. (1987), Arabic Names in the Chanson de Roland: Saracen Gods, Frankish Swords, Roland Horse, and the Olifant." Journal of the American Oriental Society. P 273.

20) Bulfinch, Thomas. 1967. Bulfinch's Mythology, Legends of Charlemagne. Lee and Shepard. Chapter 24.

21) Ross, D.J.A. (1980). Auty, Robert (ed.) Traditions of Heroic and Epic Poetry. London. Modern Humanities Research Association. p. 126.

22) Canton, William (1912). A Child's Book of Warriors. J.M Dent and Sons. "Catholic Encyclopaedia: The Holy Lance". Newadvent.org. 1 October 1910. Archived from the original on 1 January 2007. Retrieved 19 December 2013.

23) Oremus: Anglican Liturgical Library. *The Form and Order of Service that is to be performed and the Ceremonies that are to be observed in The Coronation of Her Majesty Queen Elizabeth II in the Abbey Church of St. Peter, Westminster, on Tuesday, the second day of June 1953. http://www.oremus.org/liturgy/coronation/cor1953b.html (accessed March 2021)*

CHAPTER 23

18) Crystal Wind, "Meaning and Legend of the White Deer," Blog, Crystal-wind.ca, December 18, 2014, http://www.crystalwind.ca/walking-the-red-road/meaning-and-legend-of-the-white-deer.

19) Drake Bear Stephen, March 3, 2014, https://drakebearstephen.wordpress.com/2014/03/03/hopi-prophecies/

20) Aeschylus, *The Oresteia: Agamemnon; The Libation Bearers; The Eumenides: Agamemnon, The Libation Bearers, The Eumenides (Illustrated)*, February 7th, 1984 (Penguin Classics, 1984).

21) Burian, Peter. 2011. *The Complete Aeschylus: Vol 1: The Oresteia.* Oxford University Press.

CHAPTER 24

The Foundation for the Law of Time Website: https://lawoftime.org/decode/

GRATITUDE:

1) Eric Metaxas. *Amazing Grace. William Wilberforce and the Heroic Campaign to End Slavery.* Harper Collins Publishers, 2007. p 211

REFERENCES

1. Phillips, Allan, 2019. One Mob Dreaming. https://www.onemob-dreaming.com/index.html (Recorded phone conversation, January 2020.)

2. Mythologian.net. Maltese Cross Symbol, Its Meaning, History and Relation to The Firefighter Emblem.

3. https://mythologian.net/maltese-cross-symbol-meaning-history-maltese-cross-sign-firefighter-emblem/

4. Susan Morgan Black. "The Order of Bards, Ovates and Druids," December 19, 2019. https://www.druidry.org/library/gods-goddesses/brigit.

5. Scott Alexander King. *Animal Messengers: Interpreting the Symbolic Language of the Worlds Animals.* New Holland Publishers, 2016.

6. Magenta Pixie. "Queen Sophia, Princess Aurora, the Merlin Excalibur Codex. Krystal Stargate Series Part 5)." You Tube. *The Merlin Excalibur Codex* (blog), November 25, 2019. https://youtu.be/p2UAKTGMJ10. https://www.smh.com.au/entertainment/books/the-secrets-and-dreams-of-our-first-governor-20131003-2uvlv.html)

7. Caterson, Simon. 2013. The Secrets and Dreams of our First Governor. Sydney Morning Herald.

8. Pembroke, Michael. 2013. Arthur Phillip: Sailor, Mercenary, Governor, Spy. Hardie Grant Books. p ix

9. Pembroke, Michael. 2013. Arthur Phillip: Sailor, Mercenary, Governor, Spy. Hardie Grant Books. p 148

10. Pembroke, Michael. 2013. Arthur Phillip: Sailor, Mercenary, Governor, Spy. Hardie Grant Books. p 206

11. Bruce Elder. *Blood on the Wattle*. Australia: Child & Associates Publishing Pty Ltd, 1988.

12. Monument Hill, 2020. Battle of Richmond Hill. https://monumentaustralia.org.au/themes/conflict/Indigenous/display/93434-battle-of-richmond-hill)

13. Kieza, Grantlee. 2019. Macquarie: Lover, Fighter, Egalitarian, Autocrat - The Man who Envisaged a Nation. ABC Books. Law of Time, Jose Arguelles. *Jose Arguelles at the Day Out of Time. Byron Bay, Australia*. Byron Bay, 2008.

14. Magenta Pixie: Excalibur Stargate Activations 21st December 2020. https://youtu.be/NYmgPHaaAQo

ABOUT THE AUTHOR

Artwork by Francine Commeignes -
www.blueraypaintings.com

Advanced Kinesiologist, Iridologist, Biochemical Therapist and writer Angela Sciberras (BA.Mus.hons Ethnomusicology) has been on the path to discovery of what it takes to empower human beings for most of her life, assisting her clients to get to the core of what it is that they are dealing with, and why it may be preventing them from living the life they dream.

As a clinician, therapeutic musician, workshop facilitator, public speaker, and published author, Angela combines her background as an artist with the age-old philosophy of the mystic, along with latest Neuro-Training techniques to assist clients to overcome personal blocks to success in all areas of life including business, family, health, wealth, and creativity. Angela is a qualified Neuro-Training and Neuro-Linguistic Kinesiologist who has been working with clients for over 15 years, with thousands of sessions, to empower and unleash their creative potential to achieve personal transformation, reveal and overcome personal blocks to achieving success and improve their vital health.

Angela is also a qualified Clinical Therapeutic Harpist with over 10 years' experience with thousands of clients specialising in using music to relieve pain and anxiety while bringing relaxation and peace in Palliative and Oncology Care environments. Angela now steps into what she considers to be her life's purpose, combining all her life experience into a powerful, globe-changing mission, to pass message from her ancestors who wish to pass the pain of the past onto their children's children no more.

You can connect with Angela at:
www.thekineziologist.com or www.newrealmz.com

CPSIA information can be obtained
at www.ICGtesting.com
Printed in the USA
LVHW081757210521
688148LV00017B/824